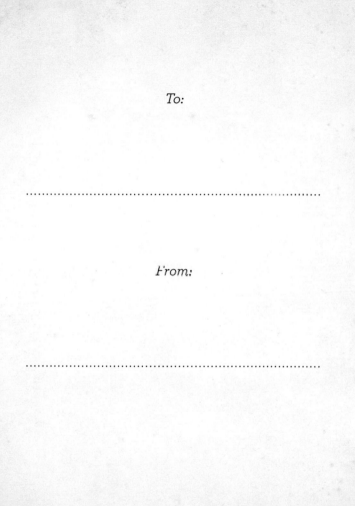

To:

....

From:

....

DEVOTIONS
from the GARDEN

DEVOTIONS
from the GARDEN

Finding Peace and Rest from Your Hurried Life

❧

with MIRIAM DRENNAN

THOMAS NELSON
Since 1798

NASHVILLE   MEXICO CITY   RIO DE JANEIRO

Published in Nashville, Tennessee, by Thomas Nelson. Thomas Nelson is a registered trademark of HarperCollins Christian Publishing, Inc.

Cover design by Alexis Ward, The Visual Republic
Front cover photo © Dariusz Gora/Shutterstock.com.
All interior images and back cover image are from Shutterstock.com.

Thomas Nelson titles may be purchased in bulk for educational, business, fund-raising, or sales promotional use. For information, please e-mail SpecialMarkets@ThomasNelson.com.

ISBN-13: 978-0-7180-3050-6

Printed in China

15 16 17 18 TIMS 5 4 3 2 1

www.thomasnelson.com

TABLE OF CONTENTS

GOD'S TRANSFORMING GRACE

*Our citizenship is in heaven, from which we also eagerly wait for the
Savior, the Lord Jesus Christ, who will transform our lowly body that
it may be conformed to His glorious body, according to the working
by which He is able even to subdue all things to Himself.*

PHILIPPIANS 3:20–24 NKJV

Perennial bulbs produce such gorgeous plants and flowers year after year that it's hard to believe their unsightly, humble beginnings.

Bulbs originate as somewhat withered-looking balls, some with fine, hairy roots extending outward, and others with crackly, dry skin. On the inside of each is a small bud, protected by those ugly outer layers. If you were to set these bulbs on a shelf, they would stay lifeless and be purposeless. But when the fall season arrives and we bury them, we set the stage for something miraculous to occur. We will witness the complete transformation of our ugly bulbs.

Upon the first hints of spring—when days are a bit longer and the snow is melting—specks of green begin to dot the soil. Each day the warmer sun coaxes and calls, "Come on! Come out!" until finally the seedlings push through the dirt, the leaves emerge, and the stage is set for the tiny flower buds to sprout and open. At long last, beautiful masterpieces open up, sharing their vibrant color for all to see. The cold ground has given birth to these explosions of joy that greet the new season.

Year after year these lovely miracles reappear. New flower buds spread rainbows of color and joy as if to remind us that they weren't asleep or dead in the ground, that they had been in a season of transformation. After being swaddled in rich soil, protected from cold winter temperatures, watered with nourishing rain, and fed with the warm, bright sun, the ugly bulbs eventually emerge as something new and beautiful, unmistakable evidence of their transformation.

Maybe you feel more like a dormant bulb than a radiant blossom. You may feel lifeless, covered in dry, crackly layers of sin as the harshness of winter bears down on you. If that's the case, take heart and find hope in God's promises for you. In due season He will clothe you in sparkling joy and renewed hope; He will trade His beauty for the apparent ashes of your life, and others will see His transformation of you, His beloved child.

If you have bulbs in your yard, dig one up today. Or buy some new ones. Before replanting them, hold each for just a moment. Consider what it will become—and remember that the Lord holds you the same way.

Father, You know that on certain days I feel lifeless,
worthless, and stale. During those times, remind me that
You are indeed at work in my life and that I will eventually
blossom, emerging for the purpose to which You call
me and spreading the joy with which You fill me.

PERENNIALS

Do not withhold Your tender mercies from me, O LORD;
Let Your lovingkindness and Your truth continually preserve me.

PSALM 40:11 NKJV

To gardeners, there is something very satisfying about perennials . . .

Every spring we wonder about the soil, the mulch, and those aspects of the garden we tended to in the winter while the plants were dormant. After the somber tones of winter, we find ourselves very ready for spring's gift of color. Never too soon the faithful and colorful perennials pop up from the ground. And when we see that certain perennials have multiplied and spread during the winter, that additional and unexpected color is truly a bonus.

Whether we plant irises, hydrangeas, roses, raspberries, or hostas, their reappearance—year after year—is a lovely illustration of God's grace and forgiveness in our lives. When we're in a spring season spiritually, we remain close to our Life Source, gathering nourishment from His hand. In a spiritual summer, we are blooming and remain steadfast; we can weather the storms and most of the droughts. But at some point our bloom fades and withers, the weeds of sin overtake us, and we find ourselves in a season of spiritual dormancy.

But think about the perennials: much is happening during their hidden existence in winter's garden. Similarly, much is happening in our soul that we don't see, but God is still very much at work. Perhaps He is softening the soil of our heart after life's hurts and disappointments have created a protective crust. Or maybe He's gently watering and loosening the soil of our heart, preparing for the seeds of a new direction, a new ministry, or a renewed excitement about our relationship with Jesus.

God is at work even in seasons of your heart that seem dormant, that lack color, and that seem to bear no fruit. Be sure that He continues to pour out His grace so that, like perennials in the garden, you will blossom again and again, adding color to the world and joy to people around you.

Precious Father, thank You that even when I feel I'm in a season of dormancy, You are not distant or idle. Instead, You are ever faithful to Your promise to work grace and renewal in my heart and my life.

NEGLECTED BEDS

Create in me a pure heart, O God,
and renew a steadfast spirit within me.

PSALM 51:10

Cleaning out a neglected bed is a dreaded task for even the biggest gardening enthusiast. As we pull out last year's overgrowth—dead weeds and vines hardened by winter—we cling to the hope that beneath it all, we'll find dark, rich soil from which new life will emerge. With the pull of each old growth, we find memories of last year's crop surfacing—some good, some not so good. There may be thoughts of those plants that produced in abundance and of others that struggled just to hang on.

Frustration can also set in as we remember why it's a good idea to clean the bed right after harvest while the soil is still soft and the vines and roots are pliable. Regret about not taking proper steps in the past in order to save time and energy in the present can easily fester. It's much more fun to start the new season by planting seedlings instead of pulling ugly, dead remains!

Maybe at this season of your life you are feeling like the neglected bed. Maybe unhealthy habits and ideas took root and took over. Maybe your heart has been hardened by the storms of winter. Maybe those seeds of hope struggled to hang on—and lost the struggle, leaving behind a sad emptiness. And maybe you're even convinced that it's too late to start over, too late to grow, flourish, and produce.

Don't underestimate the skill of your Master Gardener. He is not only willing to clean up your life, but He is able to make the soil of your heart soft and fertile again. He longs for His forgiveness and mercy to wash over you each morning like gentle rain. He is also ready to pull out what needs to be removed from your heart—and, yes, the process may be painful at times, yet the Master Gardener will then sow in you seeds of His goodness and love, preparing you once again to blossom and flourish.

God of mercy, grace, and forgiveness, thank You for untangling and weeding out the sin in my life. And thank You for planting hope where there has been pain, love where there has been bitterness, dreams where there has been brokenness. Thank You for the opportunity to grow, flourish, and produce fruit in Your name and for Your glory.

SOIL TESTING

"See what the land looks like. . . . What about the soil? Is it fertile or poor?
Are there trees there? Try to bring back some of the fruit from that land."

NUMBERS 13:18, 20 NCV

One of the first and most practical steps that gardeners can take before we plant anything is soil testing. Learning as much as possible about the soil—its texture, composition, drainage, acidity, and mineral density—will help us determine what we will have to add to the soil to help our plants thrive. Fertilizers, aluminum, lime, and other enhancers may be needed for optimal plant growth. The only way to know what to add—and how much—is to do some preliminary research.

Likewise, when God gave the land of Canaan to the Israelites, He instructed Moses to send each tribe's leader to explore the land before taking it. After all, their very survival depended on knowing the terrain. Armies trained to fight in the desert would not fare as well if they were sent to battle in the jungle. The Israelites needed to learn about their new land before they could determine which areas to establish as their own, so according to God's instruction, they did some research.

We would be wise to follow the Israelites' example and do some research when we need to make decisions that will affect our spiritual growth and productivity. If our soil is lacking in wisdom and God's truth, we are easily weakened and blinded by the ways of the world. When we seek God—when we do our research by reading His Word, getting biblical counsel from other believers, and praying for His guidance and strength—we will be prepared to make wise decisions and to accomplish all that God has for us to do. Our lives will then be a living testimony to His goodness and faithfulness.

So what's the condition of your soil? When did you last enrich your heart and mind with the living power of God's Word? How often do you slow down to listen for the Lord's divine direction for your life? He is the Master Gardener of your soul: your survival depends on Him who has everything you need to bloom and to grow beyond your wildest dreams.

Heavenly Father, I turn to You with a humble heart, seeking Your wisdom and Your way for my life. Please give me understanding and insight about _____ so I will make sound decisions based on Your guidance. Thank You for Your Word. It truly is a light to my path and a reliable source of guidance for my steps and peace for my soul.

BLUEBERRIES AND BOXWOODS

I know what it is to be in need, and I know what it is to have plenty.
I have learned the secret of being content in any and every situation,
whether well fed or hungry, whether living in plenty or in want.

PHILIPPIANS 4:12

Soil pH tends to fall into two camps: acidic or alkaline. When you know your soil's pH level, you can better determine which plants will grow well in that soil. Blueberries, for example, need an acidic soil to thrive and produce fruit, but boxwoods flourish in a more alkaline soil. Placing either plant in the other's soil would assuredly kill it. So when we garden, our goal is finding the optimum pH level for whatever we want to plant.

What about the ideal pH for our own life? Our garden may not have grown the way we had hoped. Maybe the pH was off because of our own choices or maybe because of choices made by people around us. Other people's gardens may seem to be flourishing and even pest free. But when we look at other people—whether a neighbor or a celebrity, a coworker or a family member—we don't know the pH of the soil of their lives. We don't know what challenges they face, what plants they had hoped would grow but didn't, or what plants have grown that they wish hadn't.

The reality is this: no one lives in soil with the perfect pH, a pH that enables all dreams to come true and protects from all pain and loss. When we are in Christ, however, He provides what we need to grow and produce fruit right where we are. Our earthly soil will not be perfect, but Jesus enables us to thrive in any level of acid or alkaline.

One more point. The blueberry never envies the boxwood, and the box-wood doesn't envy the blueberry. Each is content in the soil where it has been planted by a Gardener who was careful and wise. So today, rather than looking at another's growth, thank God for where He has planted you.

Master Gardener, You know that there is no perfect pH in this world, and I know that means more work for You as You grow me to be the person You want me to be. Forgive me for being envious of others who seem to be in more beautiful gardens— and teach me to live with anticipation of Your plans for me.

ALMANACS

Your word is a lamp to my feet and a light to my path.

PSALM 119:105 NKJV

Almanacs have been in the United States since the eighteenth century. Even today the still-popular Old Farmer's Almanac and Farmer's Almanac are considered highly reliable sources of information about gardening, home remedies, fishing, the moon's phases, recipes, astronomy, and weather forecasts. Since 1792, almanacs have usually had the final say after gardeners have consulted friends, neighbors, retailers, and—more recently—the Internet for information. Once they open the almanac and find exactly what they wanted to know, many gardeners wonder why they didn't consult this time-tested resource in the first place.

Too often today we treat the Bible the same way. When we need information, we poll the people we know, consult unproven sources, and sometimes find ourselves more conflicted than before we started our quest for answers and guidance. Had we first consulted the Bible and asked the Holy Spirit to guide our study, we would instead have a solid answer from a time-tested, God-breathed resource.

Granted, entire movements have arisen with their sole purpose being to disprove the Bible, to reveal it as contradictory or fabricated. But Christians are also vulnerable to abridging the Bible or distorting its truth to fit our personal, political, or social agenda. When this happens, we're not only deceiving ourselves, we are misleading others as well.

The Bible is not a random collection of isolated stories; it is purposeful and meaningful, its themes and lessons working together, always and ultimately pointing to Jesus. Instead of looking in God's Word for the answers we want to hear, let's seek instead the answers we need to hear.

Heavenly Father, thank You for setting forth Your truth in the living Word of Scripture. Thank You that Your Spirit works in concert with Your Word to guide me, grow me, and provide me with the wisdom You would have me know. I release to You those things I do not need to understand, that I will hear Your true voice more clearly.

GOD'S TIMING

The LORD is good to those who hope in him, to those who seek him. It is good to wait quietly for the LORD to save.

LAMENTATIONS 3:25-26 NCV

E very gardener has done this. Several times . . .

That first warm week in the spring arrives, and every other commercial on TV announces someone's annual spring plant sale. The bright, colorful array of flowers call our names, and before we know it, we're at the nursery. Against all logic, we snatch up as many plants as will fit in the back of our SUVs. (*After all*—we tell ourselves—*if we wait until next week, the selection will be picked over!*) Then we rush home and immediately plant our prizes, all the while hoping and praying that the weather will cooperate. Some of us—in both our excitement about the fresh, new garden and our denial of the calendar—are so proud of our early gardens that we even post photos online.

Then, even before a week goes by, another frost hits. Frantically, we drag our pots and containers inside, cover our new plants with sheets, and still lose some, if not all, of them. Then we shake our fists and vow, *"never* again!" And we keep that vow . . . until the following spring.

So what does this have to do with waiting quietly for God's timing? Everything! It is wise to wait not just when buying our spring plants, but also in our decision making and general living of life. When we're starting a business, a ministry, or a relationship, changing a job, or making a major purchase, do we take a poll of our friends, or do we pray—and then quietly wait? How often do we, in our own impatience, move full steam ahead without God's guidance or blessing?

When our impatience leads us to jump ahead of God, we cheat ourselves of His best and often live with regret that can haunt us for years. Seeking God, placing our hope in Him, and trusting His timing can be scary and down-right hard. By reminding ourselves that He has our utmost benefit at heart and quietly waiting on Him, we will better hear His voice and know His will.

Precious Father, I confess that sometimes I want something more than I want You to be a part of it. Help me always take the step of trust and make time to seek Your best for my life. Give me faith and courage to wait quietly for Your perfect timing.

DIRT UNDER YOUR FINGERNAILS

You, LORD, are our Father.
We are the clay, you are the potter;
we are all the work of your hand.

ISAIAH 64:8

It truly is one of the mysteries of gardening: Why is that one-of-a-kind feeling of having dirt under your fingernails so satisfying?

Maybe you've started an afternoon in your garden like this: your hand tools—spade, trowel, fork, rake—placed at your side, gardening gloves on your hands (after all, they're highly recommended for protection from cuts and abrasions), and rich soil waiting for your TLC. To fully experience this blessed moment, you make a conscious effort to hear the birds, take a deep breath of fresh air, smell the mustiness of the dirt, see the deep, dark soil—and see in your mind the burst of colorful vegetables and flowers that will be here one day. And that's when the thought comes: *Why am I wearing gloves?* Off they come! Now, as you get dirt underneath your fingernails, you can truly be present in your garden, not sure why it is so satisfying to dig with your hands, yet savoring the feeling and getting dirty with abandon.

Our Creator God may have had the same sort of experience when He crafted you, when He knit you together in your mother's womb (Psalm 139:13) or, to change to a dirtier metaphor, when He shaped you on His potter's wheel. Maybe you've seen a potter at work, kicking the flywheel with her foot to keep the platform turning, her hands free to work their magic, and her mind able to focus on the pot she's making. The clay is moist, leaving the same layer of dryness on a potter's hands that a gloves-free gardener knows so well.

Anything that is handmade is extra special. God crafted you with His hands, and He probably got some of that clay under His nails as He enjoyed the satisfaction of pouring His heart into the treasure He was making. Kind of like what you feel when you dig in the garden without your gloves and get dirt under your nails!

Almighty Creator God, it's inconceivable that You—who keep the planets in their orbit—knit me together; You crafted me with Your hands. Like the psalmist, I marvel that I am fearfully and wonderfully handmade by You! You got dirt under Your fingernails as You crafted one-of-a-kind me. What amazing love.

A FAMILY AFFAIR

*"Fix these words of mine in your hearts and minds. . . . Teach them to
your children, talking about them when you sit at home and when you
walk along the road, when you lie down and when you get up."*

GOD IN DEUTERONOMY 11:18–19

And when you garden!

Think about it. Gardening spans the ages, appeals to boys and girls, and, in many places, can be a year-round activity. Why not make it a special parent-child, grandparent-grandchild time for talking, laughing, digging, planting, weeding, and ultimately enjoying the fruit of your labors?

The garden can be a world unto itself—and how fun to escape to it with someone you love. The safe context can be a great place to talk about not just gardening, but whatever your child or grandchild wants to talk about. Share about the wonder of seeds, what they need to grow, and how we can partner with God in their growth. A garden reflects many aspects of life, and working together in the garden may introduce opportunities to talk and teach about the child's own physical as well as spiritual growth. What does she need to grow healthy and strong? What does he need to grow into the man of God the Lord wants him to be?

Think too of the life lessons implicit in gardening: patient waiting, consistent effort, being responsible, seeing that good things take time to unfold, understanding that work is hard but more fun when it is shared, thinking about more than yourself, and experiencing the enormous joy and satisfaction of having something grow—and then eating it!

Maybe gardening—digging in the dirt—makes you feel like a kid. Why not share the fun with a child in your life?

Lord, through the seasons I've spent in a garden, You've met me consistently, blessing me with encouragement, quietness that restores, peace, prayer time, and joy. Thank You for children with whom I can share these blessings and more. I ask that You would provide us time to garden, sweet conversations as we do, and a growing love for You and for each other as we marvel at and enjoy together this microcosm of Your amazing creation.

LANDSCAPERS VS. FARMERS VS. GARDENERS

There are different kinds of service, but the same Lord. There are different kinds
of working, but in all of them and in everyone it is the same God at work. Now
to each one the manifestation of the Spirit is given for the common good.

1 Corinthians 12:5-7

It should come as no surprise that landscapers, farmers, and gardeners often have vastly different ideas about the best use of a given patch of soil. In general, landscapers design with definition and plant for aesthetic appeal; farmers design for uniformity and plant for survival; and gardeners are usually a combination of the two, which may result in quite a bit of what I like to call "purposeful messiness."

What all three groups have in common is this: they all want to grow something. The beauty resulting from their efforts, however, may only be appreciated by the one who toiled. The landscaper is pleased when daylilies, crepe myrtle, and hostas create an appealing view, the farmer is happy when the fields produce healthy crops, and the gardener is happy when whatever was planted—flowers, herbs, fruits, vegetables—actually grows. Each one may see beauty where the others may not.

God's people are more joyful when we choose to see beauty not only in where and how we are serving, but also in the service of our fellow believers. When differences arise—when we recognize the variety of ways we minister or worship—may we celebrate the unique beauty before us. And may we learn to see beauty where we haven't seen it before.

Yes, landscapers, farmers, and gardeners approach a plot of land differently, yet a certain beauty results. May the same be true in the body of Christ as we approach differently the seed-sowing, the watering, the weeding, and the harvesting involved in our response to Jesus' Great Commission.

Lord, I confess I too often seem blind to the beauty of
your people and of the way they serve You. May I join
You in celebrating the unique abilities, passions, talents,
and ways we all serve and bring glory to You.

SOWING TO THE FLESH

Those who live according to the flesh set their minds on the things of the flesh, but those who live according to the Spirit, the things of the Spirit. . . . If you live according to the flesh you will die; but if by the Spirit you put to death the deeds of the body, you will live.

ROMANS 8:5, 13 NKJV

Most gardeners know that some plants may be sown as seeds while others will fare better as transplants. Seeds for beans, okra, corn, and cantaloupe, for example, may be planted directly into the garden, but tomatoes, eggplant, and sweet potatoes do better when they are transplanted as seedlings from their indoor beginnings.

I think it's fair to assume that no transplanting happened in the garden of Eden. Seeds simply grew as they were supposed to, and the results were beyond our imaginations. After all, Eden did not have imperfect soil or inclement weather to impede the growth of delicate shoots. In that ideal setting, seeds didn't need to be planted in one environment and then transplanted into another to improve the chances of strong and productive growth. Instead, all seeds fell onto perfect soil that enabled them to grow and thrive. But when sin entered the world, that perfect process ceased, not only in the garden but in the hearts and minds of humankind as well.

When we sow to the flesh—when we plant our desires, motives, goals, and trust in worldly matters—the crop of our life will be withered and tainted at best. Our appetites will never be satisfied, and everything that manages to grow will die. Oh, at times we may think life looks good and feels good, but it's really nothing compared to God's original plan for us.

To use gardening imagery, when we name Jesus our Savior, God transplants some of the Holy Spirit into our hearts. The Spirit's presence with us and within us enables us to sow in our lives what God intended: "love, joy, peace, longsuffering, kindness, goodness, faithfulness, gentleness, self-control" (Galatians 5:22–23 NKJV). When we plant our lives in God's perfect love, we can grow and flourish beyond anything imaginable. And His grace and forgiveness ensure that we can rip out seeds that were improperly planted and start all over again.

Father, thank You for Jesus, whose death provided the way
for me to conquer my sins and the death they bring. And
thank You for providing me the perfect conditions for turning
my mind and heart to You. And thank You for planting Your
Spirit within me that I may live a more Christlike life.

COMPANION PLANTING

Encourage one another and build each other up, just as in fact you are doing.

Compatibility can be just as important in a garden as it is in a family or a marriage, and that's what companion planting is all about.

Companion planting involves putting together in the same plot compatible plants of different species. The purpose of doing this is so the plants will help one another grow. The plants only benefit, however, if they are not in neat little rows of the same kind. Instead, the combinations are grouped together, seemingly in competition; but when they are properly paired, the plants actually depend on one another.

Tall plants provide shade for shorter plants that do not need full sun. Some strong-stalked plants may provide natural staking for viny plants like beans. Spreading plants like squash or strawberries provide nice ground cover that protects other plants from harmful pests, while other plants may attract insects beneficial to its garden companion. Certain textures of plants, like the prickly squash, deter vermin. The classic Three Sisters combination—corn, pole beans, and squash—demonstrate the positives of companion planting, as do the pairing of strawberries and peppers, roses and chives, or tomatoes and cabbage. In addition to promoting healthier gardens, companion planting also makes efficient use of land when space is at a premium.

Now think about the companion planting God has done in your marriage, your family, your church, even in your neighborhood and workplace. Each one of us has strengths and weaknesses as well as needs and wants that we cannot handle ourselves—and we're not meant to handle all of life on our own. We benefit when some of our relationships complement instead of mirror us. If, for instance, we tend to overspend, we can spend more time with friends who proactively budget their money. If we are too much of a homebody, we may need some adventurous friends to do more outdoor activities. If we are married, we can be blessed by our single friends. If we are young, we benefit from the wisdom of those who have lived longer. And if we are Christians, we can find our faith strengthened as we encourage the faith of non-Christians when we establish authentic relationships with them.

Take a moment to ask the Lord to do some companion planting in your life. Yield to His guidance so that you will be blessed as He uses you to bless others.

Lord, it is so easy and comfortable to place myself in a neat little row with like-minded people and stay there! But by doing so I may miss out on a great growth opportunity or tremendous blessing. Please guide my efforts to do some companion planting that I may grow and You might be glorified.

CROP ROTATION

Perhaps I will stay with you for a while, or even spend the winter,
so that you can help me on my journey, wherever I go.

1 CORINTHIANS 16:6

City dwellers may have heard of crop rotation—of varying the crops that are planted in a given field—but they may not know the full significance of doing so. Planting different crops in the same area keeps the soil vibrant and fertile, and disease is less likely to invade. The practice definitely takes knowledge (not all plants "take" to crop rotation) and organization (farmers need to track what was planted where), but this practice brings refreshment, replenishment, and renewal.

God's practice of moving Paul from city to city, from church to church, resulted in refreshment and renewal for believers. After his conversion, Paul traveled the ancient world, planting churches, spreading the gospel, and offering godly counsel. In addition to keeping his ministry of teaching and encouraging alive for two thousand years, Paul's epistles reveal his great love for the people he met. Although many farewells must have been gut-wrenching, Paul knew that, in His perfect timing, the Lord would move him from one field of ministry to another.

And God moves us from field to field as well. He will require us, for instance, to let go of a relationship, a job, a ministry, an adult child, or a home. These are not easy changes, and they may not be changes we would choose for ourselves. Nevertheless, for reasons we might never understand, we must let go; we must move on so the Gardener can grow us as well as the people whose lives we touch.

One more thought. If Paul had remained in his hometown of Tarsus and established a church, we might not have the New Testament today. After all, it's comprised of letters he wrote to churches he loved. Paul never abandoned the Galatians, the Ephesians, or the Corinthians. He kept in touch, sometimes visiting, and always caring about the individuals as well as the body of Christ as a whole. Throughout his years as God's servant, Paul remained open to rotation, to going where the Lord led, and trusting in His purposes.

Father, forgive me when I agonize over an unwanted change in my life. Forgive me when I try to fix the situation or hold on to the circumstances when You intend for me to rotate, to let go, to move on. Help me keep my heart and soul open to wherever You will lead me next, knowing that such rotations mean vibrant spiritual health.

GRACE IN THE GARDEN

*Perhaps the reason [your runaway slave Onesimus] was separated from
you for a little while was that you might have him back forever . . .
The grace of the Lord Jesus Christ be with your spirit.*

PHILEMON VV. 15, 25

ardening can be confusing at times, especially when you're a total rookie
and even if you're experienced and dealing with a new climate or a new-
to-you plant. And most of us have more than one kind of plant in our gardens.
So determining the right amount of sun, fertilizer, and soil for each one, not
to mention remembering each plant's maturity timeline, can be challenging, if
not completely confusing. So we make mistakes, we use incorrect techniques,
we put on wrong amounts of fertilizer, but then something amazing happens!
Fruit emerges, vegetables grow, and flowers bloom. Despite our mistakes, we
actually reap a harvest! That's grace!

You may never have thought of that word as a gardening term, but it definitely fits. *Grace* is undeserved, unearned, unmerited favor. It's a shoot that
sprouts despite our sporadic watering. It's fruit growing even though we didn't
ever quite figure out how to keep the bugs away.

On a more significant level, grace is God remaining faithful when we have
turned away from Him. Grace is God's forgiveness of our sins when we confess
that we've messed up. God's grace has us covered despite all our human stum-
blings, our sinful choices, and our selfish attitudes.

Besides responding with gratitude and thanksgiving, we are to share God's
grace with others. Sometimes that means telling someone about Jesus. Sometimes sharing God's grace means forgiving someone—just as Philemon had the

opportunity to forgive the now-Christ-following Onesimus for stealing from him and then running away. Not an easy assignment for Philemon! You may also be facing a difficult opportunity to forgive. Look again at the cross, realize that your sin put Jesus there, thank Him for forgiving you, and ask Him to help you forgive the person you need to forgive.

Then do something we can never do too much of: spend some time thanking God for His truly amazing grace. After all, He will receive us, forgive us, cleanse us, and accept us no matter how many times we get it wrong.

That's grace!

Father God, thank You for Your amazing grace, Your faithful love, Your ready forgiveness, Your constant presence with me, Your guiding and teaching Spirit, Your written Word, and the Living Word, Your Son and my Savior, Jesus Christ. All of this—and more—is grace!

THE MANTIS

Hear the sound of my prayer,
when I cry out to you for help.
I raise my hands
toward your Most Holy Place.

PSALM 28:2 NCV

The mantis is an interesting and fascinating creature. Consider, for instance, why its name has two possible spellings. With its front legs in the position they are, a mantis does indeed appear to be *praying*. What a kindred spirit for those gardeners who find themselves praying to God, listening for His voice, and learning lessons from the soil! But all gardeners appreciate the *preying* that this insect does. Its diet consists primarily of aphids, leafhoppers, and mosquitoes, but the larger, more mature mantis has been known to capture small scorpions, frogs, and rodents. Clearly the garden as well as the gardener benefit from the presence of the *praying/preying* mantis.

The homonymic name of this valuable insect also offers insight about an authentic relationship with God. Many times, as Christ's followers, we still pursue our own desires and, in doing so, become prey for the enemy. Telling ourselves that we can always ask for forgiveness later, we plunge deeper and deeper into our own cravings. To paraphrase St. Augustine, the ear of our hearts is deafened by the din of our vanities.* We *prey on* our pursuits instead of *praying about* them—and, intent on this path leading away from our Lord, we become *prey* to the enemy.

---

* *The Confessions of St. Augustine*, Book IV

So every day and sometimes every hour, we need to pray. Daily communion with God serves as our armor; ongoing prayer is our direct line to His power, guidance, and wisdom. During times of prayer, we learn to recognize His voice as we seek His will.

So today, will you *pray*—or will you become *prey*?

Holy Spirit, reveal to me any selfish pursuits or self-righteous behaviors; they are not from You, and I seek forgiveness. As I go about my day, may I remain in a state of ongoing prayer. I need You every second that I breathe.

SEED CLEANING

Who can understand his errors?
Cleanse me from secret faults.

PSALM 19:12 NKJV

When's the last time you grew a tomato that tasted like a tomato? Or a delicious, velvety squash that melted in your mouth? If you hoped to replicate those same results year after year, you may have saved the seeds.

Called seed cleaning, this very old practice was used by farmers who wanted consistent results. But during the twentieth century, the practice faded as a result of commercial seed companies, corporate farms, and legislation. With today's renewed interest in clean organic food, however, gardeners are reinstituting the practice. This renaissance of seed cleaning means that people are learning what certain foods are supposed to taste like!

The seed-cleaning process varies depending on whether the seed is wet or dry, and seed cleaning will not work if it's not done properly or if the seed is not truly cleaned. If any shred of pulp or chaff remains, the seed may lose its vigor or die.

That pulp or chaff impacts a seed much the way our "secret faults" impact us: we may lose our spiritual vigor and our passion for God may die. That pulp or chaff operates much like the secret faults referred to in today's psalm. How often do we sin without really understanding why? How often do we serve or give with wrong or selfish motives?

Jesus does not want us to worry and stay guilt-stricken over what we may be doing wrong or what we have done wrong. When the time is right, His Spirit will convict us so that we can confess our sin and receive forgiveness.

Back to our garden. The next time you're slicing a tomato, try separating one of the seeds, and you'll see that it's virtually impossible. And it is utterly impossible for you to separate your guilt from yourself, but Jesus has taken care of that. So hand off to Him any guilt you are holding onto. Release your heart into His hands. Find in His cleansing not only joy but also vigor for your walk of faith.

Father God, I am guilty of holding on to _____. Free me from its hold on me. Wash me in Your grace and forgiveness.

THE SPARK OF LIFE

"As the heavens are higher than the earth,
so are my ways higher than your ways
and my thoughts than your thoughts."

Isaiah 55:9

Seeds come in a variety of shapes, sizes, and colors, yet within each is a rather mysterious spark of life that God has placed in each seed. That spark awakens with the right amount of water, the right nutrients, the right temperature, and according to its own right time frame.

It's exciting to know we as gardeners play a role in the awakening of the spark. We are attentive to the water and nutrients, we plant at the right time of year, we remain sensitive to temperatures, and we wait. We trust that our active waiting—our faithful fulfillment of our gardening duties—will awaken that spark and that, one day, that seed will come to life, send forth a shoot, and break through the earth. We live with the mystery in sure anticipation of the celebration.

God gives us similar opportunities to live with mystery, to actively wait for His perfect timing, and to choose to confidently anticipate His good and perfect answers to our prayers. In fact, God leaves room for us to choose to trust Him with every aspect of our lives and our futures through faith. He desires for us to draw nearer to Him to learn more about Him, to know His peace, and to experience His blessing. When we do, broken relationships, lost careers, addictions, and loss—events that might have devastated us in an earlier spiritual season—no longer plunge us into despair. And praiseworthy moments—a check that arrives at just the right time, an encouraging word when we need it most, or even the simple pleasure of a beautiful spring morning—we more readily recognize as gifts from the Lord. Such moments of celebration fuel the fire of trust in our heavenly Father.

So today, embrace what you do not understand about God's ways and His timing. Let the unknown and the mysterious compel you to trust God that this is an opportunity—in His perfect time—for you to grow, for you to better see, trust, and love Him.

Lord God, I can enjoy a good mystery novel because I can peek and see how it ends. I don't always enjoy the mystery of the unseen future: I can't peek and see the specifics. So may Your faithfulness, goodness, wisdom, power, and love enable me to live with the mystery of how and when You'll answer my prayers, and enable me to live with confident anticipation of Your blessing.

NATURE'S PLOW

Better to be of a humble spirit with the lowly,
Than to divide the spoil with the proud.

PROVERBS 16:19 NKJV

The lowly earthworm is a welcome sight to a gardener, for earthworms are the caretakers of a garden's foundation: the soil.

Soil that is rich in earthworms is rich indeed, and here's why. As they crawl around underground, earthworms push the soil with their heads, allowing more air and moisture to circulate through the soil. They quietly work to till and plow, opening up passages that help sprouting seeds penetrate the surface. Their excrement—called "casings"—adds even more nourishment to the soil. And the rich results give every kind of seed planted a better chance of thriving.

Yet, while these lowly creatures are hard at work enriching the soil, they are rarely noticed by those of us who will ultimately benefit from their labor. And all of us know people who, like these noble earthworms, work day after day, quietly and diligently. Maybe they are administrators or volunteers; perhaps they are neighbors, child care workers, clerks, or custodians. They help provide a strong foundation for everyday existence; they keep organizations running and have no desire for the spotlight. Their impact is significant, but we too often overlook their contributions as we celebrate our successes. These workers aren't seeking a public spotlight. Instead, these humble workers appreciate a simple, heartfelt "thank you" from someone they have supported.

Think about people like these whom you have been with or are today blessed to know. Pray for their hearts, for their hopes and their dreams, which they've probably never shared with you. Thank God for these dear folks who have chosen and continue to choose to quietly serve and support you—and make a point of letting them know personally how much you appreciate them.

Lord, when I stop to think about the people who've helped improve the soil for my spiritual growth and those who nourish that growth even today, I clearly see Your presence in each one. Thank You for putting these precious people into my life during just the right seasons. Bless them— each and every one—with people who will support and love them just as they have supported and loved me.

GERMINATION

[Ananias] stood beside me and said, "Brother Saul, receive your
sight!" And at that very moment I was able to see him.

Then he said: "The God of our ancestors has chosen you to know his will
and to see the Righteous One and to hear words from his mouth."

<small>ACTS 22:13–14</small>

Gardeners rarely see that moment when a seed comes to life, buried as it is beneath a protective layer of loamy, richly prepared soil. That first spark of energy is a deeply private moment between Creator and creation. But when the seedling sends forth its first shoot from its hidden home, the gardener will celebrate.

In the Christian life, many of our germinating moments may be private too. Think about that precise moment when you first believed . . . when God helped you understand a truth you had been wrestling with . . . when you heard His voice for the first time . . . or when His presence pierced your heart and His love became unquestionably personal. Moses had germinating moments like these. David certainly had them, as did Paul. In the Christian life, these delicate, sweet moments take us deeper in our relationship with Jesus, expand our understanding of His character and purpose, and align our thinking, our values, and our priorities with His. We are never the same.

As you and I draw closer to Christ through the seasons of life, He will entrust us with more wisdom, grant us the strength we need to serve Him in greater ways, heighten our sensitivity to the Spirit's guidance, and make us more and more like Him. Just as a seed reaches a point when it can no longer contain its contents—the point when it must burst apart in order to grow—God's people burst forth with life in Him.

May we celebrate those moments of germination. May we take a moment to thank the Father and savor His enveloping presence. Sing and clap your hands . . . or smile and enjoy the holy quiet. After all, this is a deeply personal, deeply private moment between Creator and creation.

Precious Father, thank You for sending Jesus to provide a way for You and me to be in relationship with each other. Thank You for pursuing me, for calling me to You, and revealing Yourself to me. Because of Your amazing grace, I will never be the same.

REPELLERS

*You, Lord, will keep the needy safe
and will protect us forever from the wicked.*

Psalm 12:7

Citronella, lemongrass, purple artist ageratum, marigolds—these are just a few of the plants that naturally repel pests like mosquitoes and nematodes and keep them from destroying the more vulnerable plants in the garden. Gardeners know to include such plants alongside their vegetables, fruits, and cutting flowers.

When we hear the word *repeller*, though, we might automatically conclude that the plant is ugly and has a foul smell. But some repellers actually emit a lovely fragrance, produce colorful blooms, and make great container arrangements for a patio or porch. Even when they're pleasant to have around, these repellers do their job well. In fact, although many effective synthetic pesticides are available today, none can compare to the ones provided by God Himself.

Like our backyard gardens, we often need repellers in the garden of our lives. Among our choices are friends, mentors, and family members who give us godly counsel, hold us accountable, and help us avoid going down a wrong path or making a choice we would regret. God may send some for the sole purpose of keeping us sharpened. They may be a Bible study teacher, a church elder, or wise confidant we trust with our spiritual health and growth. All the repellers God puts in your life, however, are tangible evidence that He loves you enough to provide guidance and protection during times of difficulty, doubt, decision making, or when the enemy is on the attack.

Think of one person who has been an effective repeller in your life. Take time to thank him or her for the role he or she played and the significant difference that person made in your life. Be as specific as you can about the land mines their godly counsel has helped you avoid.

While you're at it, plant a few marigolds or ageratum in your garden, not just to keep away pests, but also to remind you of your loving God's role of repeller in your life.

Holy Father, thank You for _____ _____. Thank You for the time, wisdom, and encouragement they've given me. Help me never to take them for granted. And help me either return the favor or help others in the same way they have helped me. In fact, reveal to me anyone who may need me to be a repeller—and then enable me to be effective.

SUN EXPOSURE

Your word is a lamp for my feet,
a light on my path.

PSALM 119:105

While the amount and type required may vary, all plants require sun exposure to grow. Light energy is essential to creating the sugars and starches that sustain the plant. Even on the cloudiest of days, a few minutes of sunlight peeking through is better than if the plant were placed in a dark corner.

The same can be said about spending time in God's Word each day. Of course, schedules are full, life's circumstances create cloudy conditions, we enter into seasons when we want to give up, and eventually we find ourselves in a dark corner, thinking for whatever reason that this is as good as life gets. Oh, our vision adjusts to the darkness, but we never really see clearly. And sometimes we don't see God's truth at all. We need light. We need *His* light.

No wonder, standing in the dark each day, we find our spirits getting depleted and needing to be fed. Your choice of spiritual nourishment may differ significantly from the next person's choice, and that's fine. Getting the nourishment is what matters! You may spend an hour with Him each morning before the sun comes up or at night before you crawl into bed. You may open the Bible or pray during five-minute intervals throughout the day. You may only have time to read a single verse now and ponder it later. And in some seasons of life you should definitely count ten minutes of solitude with Him as a victory—because it is! Even a few minutes with the Almighty God—with your Good Shepherd—and His Word will provide nourishment for your spirit. And as you find yourself hungrier for more, know that He will gladly provide.

For now, for today, for this moment, make the commitment to spend time with God each day. However this happens isn't as important as making it happen. We can't grow spiritually if we don't go to the food Source that God provided: our spirits are starving and can only be satisfied by Him.

Besides, a few minutes of Sonlight peeking through life's clouds is better than spending a day in the dark.

Lord, forgive me for the days—the times—when I prefer darkness to Your light. Forgive me for the times I think, "I've got this!" And thank You for moments like this one, moments in Your light, when I recognize that I need both You and Your Word to guide me, feed me, and lead me.

PINCHING AND DEADHEADING

We are hard pressed on every side, but not crushed; perplexed, but not in
despair; persecuted, but not abandoned; struck down, but not destroyed.

2 Corinthians 4:8–9

How often do you find yourself muttering, "I take three steps forward . . . and two steps back"? You may be talking about your finances, parenting skills, dating, career, health, or other goals you're working toward. The setbacks are usually unexpected; they may or may not be catastrophic. But they can be embarrassing, and they're usually discouraging. When you experience a setback, do you give up or start over? Let's see what the garden teaches.

Fruit-producing plants like strawberries benefit from pinching off the first-season blooms. No, the plants won't look very good, but by pinching them—and, yes, sacrificing most of the fruit that first year—the plants will yield significantly more fruit in subsequent seasons. On the other hand, plants like roses benefit from deadheading—from removing the old, dead flowers—so that they do *not* produce their fruit, known as rose hips. While not as severe as pruning, the acts of pinching and deadheading allow plants to mature, reenergize, and fulfill their purpose with even greater strength and vitality the following season. But during that first season, each plant looks rather unsightly and even lifeless.

Now consider that when you find yourself hard-pressed, perplexed, or struck down, God may be pinching or deadheading your life. Perhaps you are within His will, and He will use that setback to prepare you for something far greater than your expectations. Or, if God is deadheading, maybe He is trying to get your attention: parts of your life have not been aligned with His will, and He wants you to address those and get back on track.

Regardless of the type of setback, Paul assured us that we will not be destroyed: Jesus is with us. No matter how grim our situation, we have our Savior who will never leave us, never forsake us. He will give us the fortitude we need to endure His pinching and deadheading, actions He takes to enable us to be healthy and fruitful.

Lord Jesus, thank You for showing me how much You care
about my life: You take the time to either pinch or deadhead
my actions and attitudes, my goals and decisions. I know
You do this only because You love me. Thank You.

GRAFTED TO HIM

Consider therefore the kindness and sternness of God: sternness to those [people of Israel] who fell, but kindness to you [Gentiles], provided that you continue in his kindness. Otherwise, you also will be cut off. And if they do not persist in unbelief, they will be grafted in, for God is able to graft them in again.

ROMANS 11:22–23

Grafting is the joining together of tissue from two or more plants to form a new plant, and it is a fascinating but extremely slow process. Sometimes, for various reasons, grafting doesn't work, but when it does, the result is usually a stronger, more productive plant that is more resistant to pests and infection.

Grafting calls for a very specific cut on the branches or shoots being joined together, and the most successful grafts happen when those cuts fit together perfectly. By God's design, the branches heal, and the entire plant or tree is actually made stronger. While the precision of the cuts and the resulting fit contribute to the success of a graft, it is still a miraculous mystery when the two plants join together to form a single plant. And in this process God offers us a beautiful picture of grace. Grafting is also a picture of the work of grace God does within each believer.

When we first decide to turn to God, our decision may be sincere, half-hearted, or perhaps even skeptical. But when we choose to open our hearts and minds to God's truth, He grafts us to Himself—and His grafts never fail. Joined with God we are made whole—we are stronger, more productive, and more resistant to temptations that may have previously infected us.

*Precious Father, thank You for Your grace, by which
You have spiritually grafted me into the body of Christ
where I am strengthened by Your Spirit. Please protect
my heart and mind so that I may not fall away, that
my graft will stay firm, that I will be strong in You.*

NATIVE PLANTS

Each one is tempted when he is drawn away by his own desires and enticed.

JAMES 1:14 NKJV

There is a growing interest among landscaping enthusiasts to use native plants—those that grow naturally in a particular area—when they design their gardens. This trend not only benefits the local ecosystem, but the landscape itself stands a better chance of surviving.

You see, God gave us a beautiful world of plants and flowers to celebrate and enjoy, but He was very particular about where He put each kind. Colorful and majestic tropical flowers, for example, would probably not survive the cold winters of Maine. A tree that thrives in Japan may bring disease or drive away pollinating insects in Alabama. Some of these nonnative species could also wreak havoc on allergy sufferers. Have you ever thought about that fact? How could a magnificent flowering tree be the source of plant disease or our sniffles? Surely something so colorful and lovely—something we insist on having in our yards—couldn't be the cause of so much distress! . . . Or could it?

Like disease- or insect- or pollen-bearing plants, sin often enters our lives wrapped in a delightful, enticing package. We may even insist that something so lovely be part of our lives. And, yes, its presence can cause immeasurable distress.

That being the case, ask God to reveal sin's presence in your life. It may be wrapped in the pretty package of materialism, an ungodly relationship, or something that doesn't necessarily look like sin to anyone but you and the Lord. Stand firm in your faith that His ways are for your own good, stay open to what God reveals to you about yourself, and be willing to make the necessary changes because you trust in Him. It may be time to remove something pretty and replace it with something healthy.

> *Lord Jesus, thank You for reminding me that not all lush plants and colorful flowers are the best choices for my garden—and that sometimes, no matter how attractive and enticing, beautiful things in my life are not always a good choice for me. Lord, I know what I am asking You to do might be painful, but please reveal to me—and help me remove—whatever is not native to my soul.*

ENGINEERED HOLINESS

"Those who teach their own ideas are trying to get honor for themselves. But those who try to bring honor to the one who sent them speak the truth, and there is nothing false in them."

JESUS IN JOHN 7:18 NCV

In the past century, not only has the produce we buy changed but so has where we buy it. Vegetable stands set up by local gardeners have been displaced by air-conditioned stores with their larger, more colorful displays and a wider variety of fruit and vegetables. Today's consumers also demand prettier food, so scientists have engineered ways to make fruits and vegetables bigger, brighter, shinier. And less flavorful. And, in certain cases, downright harmful.

We, however, are limited in what we can do to improve food. We can modify, enhance, cross-germinate, and display like crazy, but only God can create. Only God can make something from nothing. And one amazing thing God creates is an authentic faith in us if we abide in Him.

Some of God's most faithful followers quietly work unnoticed, but other believers like the attention their service attracts. Instead of authentic worship and heartfelt preaching, some believers instead perform and offer pep talks that draw more attention to themselves than to God. Genuine believers, however, live a life that points people to Jesus, their Savior and Lord.

Whom does your faith—the way you live out your faith—draw attention to? Jesus? Or yourself? It's difficult to look into this mirror; it's a difficult admission and an even more difficult confession when we see pride in our reflection. Yet that is the kind of truth that sets us free. So if you need to, take the first step and open your heart before God. Then ask Him to grow in you a faith that can withstand seasons of plenty and times of want; a faith that seeks only to do His will and please Him; a faith that is not enhanced or modified by any other person, the culture, or new ideas. Created by God Himself, we find satisfaction and fulfillment only when we are fed by His hands. Not our own. Not anyone else's. His hands . . . that were pierced for us.

Lord Jesus, I've realized that I can too easily try to fill a spiritual void by seeking people's attention and gaining their approval. I know that You understand my need for affirmation. May I seek that affirmation –and find it—in You and in You alone.

MULCH AND ROOT FLARES

As Solomon grew old, his wives caused him to follow other gods. He
did not follow the LORD completely as his father David had done.

1 KINGS 11:4 NCV

M ulch is a gardener's friend.

Usually applied twice a year, mulch insulates perennials for the winter, protects them from weeds in the summer, and provides a polished, finished look to any landscape. But when novice landscapers and gardeners build mulch rings that bury a tree's root flare—the part of the trunk that flares into the tree's root system—they are inadvertently suffocating the tree. Whatever size the tree, its root flare needs to be exposed so that the feeder roots will grow laterally to both take in and release the gases needed for the tree's optimal health and growth. If lateral growth causes suffocation for these feeder roots, they'll grow upward, eventually encircling the tree's base and strangling it. So even though building mulch rings around the root flare is intended to provide an advantage for a long, healthy life, doing so can actually cost the tree its very existence.

And that is a picture of the life of Solomon. Perhaps the wisest man who ever lived, he had asked God for wisdom when he could have asked for anything, and God provided abundantly. And because Solomon chose wisdom, God also gave him great wealth and prosperity. Even today, Solomon's teachings and insights into both the human condition and our need for God's wisdom continue to be relevant.

Solomon's less-than-wise lifestyle, however, led to his demise. Having taken in more than one thousand wives and concubines, Solomon was influenced by their pagan cultures and idolatrous practices. He allowed these worldly influences to cover his root-flare connection to God.

Like Solomon, we are surrounded by wayward and enticing influences, yet retreating from the world with all its temptations is not an option for those who follow Jesus. We are to reach out to people of different cultures and traditions, befriending them and, ideally, finding an opportunity to share the gospel with them.

As we live in this world of many cultures and wide-ranging beliefs, the best way to protect our root flare is to remain grounded in God's Word and connected to fellow believers who will hold us accountable to live according to God's standards. Then, insulated by Scripture, we can continue to live for the Lord, bearing the fruit of His Spirit and being available to share the truth of the gospel.

Lord God, help me recognize what may be stifling my growth in You. I want the protection of Your Word; I want to be wise when I hear untruths presented as truth; and I want You to use me to share Your gospel truth that sets people free.

PRUNING

"[My Father] cuts off every branch in me that bears no fruit, while every branch that does bear fruit he prunes so that it will be even more fruitful."

JESUS IN JOHN 15:2

Pruning is a good way to promote a healthy garden: this cutting off of dead leaves, blossoms, stems, and branches helps give a plant shape and, more important, encourages growth. (In fact, trimmings cut from certain plants can grow on their own, independent of the source plant from which they were cut.) The longer this vital step of pruning is delayed, however, the more difficult these benefits will take to occur. Furthermore, pruning is a delicate process: if done incorrectly, it can actually kill a plant instead of promote its growth.

Spiritual pruning works the same way. God will cut away something or someone who is keeping us from growing. This pruning can mark the beginning of a dark period because the sources of comfort and strength we've relied on are gone. Making the darkness heavier is the fact that God seems so far away. Whatever the specifics of this very personal process, pruning means the removal of hindrances that keep us from becoming all that we can be in God's plan for our lives.

Being pruned is never fun, comfortable, or pleasant, yet when the process is completed—when unhealthy parts of our character have been removed—our life can take on a new shape, and we can find ourselves growing spiritually with new vitality. Then, relying more on God's power and strength, we move forward in life in ways that are pleasing to Him and beneficial to us and others.

Father God, I often ask myself, "Why is this happening to me?" when, in fact, I should be asking You, "What are You trying to teach me?" When You need to remove something from my life—particularly something I don't want to release—remind me that this pruning is necessary for my spiritual health, growth, and well-being.

PAINTBRUSH POLLINATION

He who turns a sinner from the error of his way will save
a soul from death and cover a multitude of sins.

JAMES 5:20 NKJV

S ometimes male and female plants need a little assistance with the pollination process. The plants may be somewhat incompatible or not attractive to nature's pollinators. The latter is the case for paw-paw trees: honeybees and butterflies are not attracted to these trees. So paw-paws don't get pollinated unless another source comes along to help—such as paintbrushes. Let me explain . . .

If you ever-so-delicately dip the tip of a small paintbrush inside the bloom of one plant and then into the bloom of another of the same species, you will pollinate the plants. Repeat this process with each bloom—using a new brush for each species of plant—to exchange their pollens. This process is never as efficient and accurate as the work of the honeybee, but it gets the job done enough so that each plant benefits.

James described a similar course of action for us when we see a fellow believer who has strayed from his or her faith. It's vital for us to take the time and care to—in love—steer that person back toward God. We can invite them back to church, welcome them into our homes for dinner, or meet at a coffee house to catch up on each other's lives. We don't have the power to change anyone's heart, but we can help steer him or her back to the One who does. God can use us to "save a soul from death." In fact, there is no limit to what God can do as His people spread His love one touch at a time.

*Lord, when I see a believer who has strayed from faith in You,
guide my actions and give me the words that You can use
to encourage them to return to You. Remove all judgment
from my heart so that I extend a gentle, honest, and sincere
spirit of love. Bless my efforts so that this person, Your child,
will be restored, for his or her good and for Your glory.*

ROOT SYSTEMS

Blessed is the one who trusts in the LORD
whose confidence is in him.
They will be like a tree planted by the water
that sends out its roots by the stream.
It does not fear when heat comes;
its leaves are always green
It has no worries in a year of drought
and never fails to bear fruit.

JEREMIAH 17:7–8

For the most part, a root system is unseen. Its underground job is to anchor the plant, store energy, seek water, and both absorb and send nutrients to the shoot it supports. In essence, roots are vital to a plant's survival. Depending on the type of plant, roots will push deep down into the soil or spread out horizontally from just a few inches to several feet. Root systems can be very intricate, some even forming patterns such as a jellyfish or a starburst or spider; some look like spinning tops or fans. Whatever they look like, these root systems—vital to a plant's survival—need to be healthy, and that means undisturbed, so they can absorb the nutrients and water the plant needs. Poor soil drainage, the presence of weeds, a lack of minerals, and underground pests can all attack, poison, and even destroy an otherwise healthy root system.

Now consider your own root system. What anchors you? What nutrients are available, and where do you find life-giving water? Your family, church, friends, community, and coworkers; your time being quiet with God, reading the Bible, worshipping, listening to music, watching TV—these either feed and fortify your spiritual growth, or deplete and rob you of your spiritual health.

Unlike plants, we are able to care for and protect our root system. We can't depend on someone else. So how are your roots doing? Have you sunk them deep into the fertile soil of God's Word? Do they drink deeply of His truth and His instruction? Is your home a place where you grow in your knowledge of Him and productively serve family members? Are you edified by healthy friendships and a healthy church? Do you seek wise counsel from trusted mentors?

As you consider your life today, what are you doing to develop and preserve the strongest root system possible? Your root system is the foundation of your life. Make sure your roots are supplying all that you need to grow in your knowledge of and love for your Lord Jesus.

Holy Spirit, help me accurately see how healthy my roots are or aren't. Also, teach me to care for them properly. Help me nourish them with Your Word, that I may grow strong and tall, able to serve with energy and bring glory to You.

ROOT ROT

You have put the evil people here
like plants with strong roots.
They grow and produce fruit.
With their mouths they speak well of you,
but their hearts are really far away from you.

JEREMIAH 12:2 NCV

Even when a root system anchors a plant, stores energy, and both absorbs and conducts nutrients, the plant's growth doesn't always go according to plan. For various reasons, for instance, a gardener sometimes has to disturb a root system, and timing is critical. Pulling weeds before a cultivated plant has developed its own strong root system can be very detrimental. But more sinister than easy-to-spot weeds is the enemy called root rot.

Usually caused by fungi, roundworms, and disease-causing microorganisms, root rot really takes hold when soil drainage is poor and the root rot has gone unnoticed for some time. Once the symptoms are visible, it's usually too late to restore the plant. It has been ill for a long time before its leaves yellow, the stem withers, and the shoots waste away. Root rot is hidden, silent, and deadly.

Like any gardener, Jeremiah clearly saw the weeds and was troubled by them, but he didn't necessarily concentrate on the root rot being caused by the smooth-talking false prophets of his day. God was concerned about both—the obvious weeds and the root rot of those who spoke words of allegiance to Him but who did not reverence Him in their hearts. The destructive presence of the latter is far more difficult to both identify and combat.

Today, are we distracted by the obvious weeds of our culture, false religions, and the increasing slide away from Christian values? Are we therefore missing the more subtle danger presented by individuals who speak Jesus' name, who have followers, but who themselves don't know the Jesus of the Bible or follow Him?

In order to have a strong spiritual foundation, we need to be rooted in God's Word, His teachings, His strength, and His grace. And only a strong spiritual foundation like this will enable us to discern sources of spiritual disease that include many famous authors, speakers, celebrities, events, musicians, movements, leaders, and churches.

In the face of these threats to God's followers, trust His promise to draw near to you as you draw near to Him (James 4:8).

Holy Spirit, help me strengthen and protect my root system so that nothing will harm it. May I leave the false teachers in God's hands and instead focus on drawing near to You.

FRUIT TREES

Trust in the LORD with all your heart
and lean not on your own understanding;
in all your ways submit to him,
and he will make your paths straight.

PROVERBS 3:5–6

For at least the first two years, fruit trees are the most high-maintenance plant we can choose to grow. The kind of fruit doesn't matter; all fruit trees demand from a gardener at least two years of high-level maintenance. I suppose it helps that most fruit trees are beautiful, and they have lovely, often fragrant, blooms that attract bees. And if you manage to protect your fruit trees from disease, to avoid canker, to repel pests, and to prune them properly, the rewards are, literally, the fruit of your efforts. Simple, right? Not exactly—and especially not at the start.

And it's not just a fruit tree that benefits from extra attention in the beginning. Anything and everything new—a new marriage, a new friendship, a new job, a new baby—will also benefit from our extra attention, from our deliberate investment of energy, time, prayer, and love in the beginning. According to Deuteronomy 24:5, for instance, a newly married man "must not be sent to war or have any other duty laid on him. For one year he is to be free to stay at home and bring happiness to the wife he has married." This year was a time for laying a solid relational foundation for the years to come.

Like the first years of a marriage, the start of a child's life is key to—among many fundamentals—a sense of being lovable and loved, a sense of worth, a discovery of their world and whether it is safe. Early stages of a friendship are times to establish trust, integrity, respect, and mutuality.

How do you lay a solid foundation when you've never been married before, you've never raised a child—or this child—before, when you are getting to know someone? You turn to the Lord—and continue to turn to the Lord—in His Word and in prayer for wisdom and guidance. He wants to bless you with a fulfilling marriage, with children who love Him and will choose to walk with Him, and with godly friends who help you grow to be more like Jesus. God will provide. And you can be confident that investing time and effort on the front end will yield strength and blessings.

Holy Spirit, sometimes I struggle to welcome change. Give me wisdom at the start of something new so that, by Your power and for Your glory, I am a good steward of the opportunity.

SUCCESSION PLANTING

Each of you must bring a gift in proportion to the
way the LORD your God has blessed you.

DEUTERONOMY 16:17

Ever find yourself eating your homegrown tomatoes for breakfast, lunch, dinner, and dessert? Or maybe you have so much yellow squash that you can't make enough casseroles before it begins to rot?

While it's fun for gardeners to share their abundance with neighbors, coworkers, and fellow church members, some gardeners practice succession planting in order to prevent an overabundance at a single harvest time. Succession planting cuts down on crop gluttony and, long term, can actually mean a greater yield overall. When gardeners plant the same crop at different intervals, one crop has just been sown while another is ripe for picking. Consider what this concept of succession planting suggests about our financial giving to the church.

Most of us do not have the ability to give a huge sum of money with a single check. As with succession planting, though, giving smaller amounts regularly has certain advantages. When we give the same smaller amount every month, for instance, our church may begin to count on us and move our gift from the "variable" column to the "budgeted" column. More importantly, though, when we give the same smaller amount at a given interval, we regularly remind ourselves that all we have—including our income—is God's and is from God. We regularly choose to trust God by giving away some of what He has provided for us. And we regularly strengthen our faith as we witness once again His great faithfulness to us: we have enough—if not more than enough—despite what we gave away.

Storing up treasures of this earth suggests that we aren't trusting God to provide for our needs. So, today, let's exercise and strengthen our faith muscle by giving what we can, choosing to trust that God will provide what we need. Whom will you bless today as you give financially—and, at the same time, give God an opportunity to grow your faith in Him?

Lord, help me overcome both my fear of not having enough and my thinking that what I have to give is not enough to make a difference. Reassure me that my gifts do help, particularly when they are joined with other people's gifts. Father, as I choose to trust Your promise to provide for me, may I give freely and joyfully.

RAINY DAYS

Ask the LORD for rain in the springtime;
it is the LORD who sends the thunderstorms.
He gives showers of rain to all people,
and plants of the field to everyone.

ZECHARIAH 10:1

Rainy days can kill plans quickly, can't they? They cancel ball games, hikes, picnics, even outdoor work. Figuratively speaking, rainy days are life's bad experiences or trying times. We tend to favor sunshine over rain, whether it's in our hearts or our backyards.

But gardeners welcome rainy days as a respite from watering. They know that no sprinkler or hose nourishes a flower bed the way God's rain does. When it falls on plants, rain revives, rejuvenates, and sustains life. It's just as essential to the growth and health of a plant as the sun is.

No wonder gardeners and farmers pray for rain, but it seems unlikely that we would ever pray for rain in our lives. During rainy seasons, though, we who have parched hearts have the opportunity to soak in God's Spirit and let Him have His way in us. In fact, such seasons are essential to our growth and health. A good rainy season can awaken us, test us, and turn us to God. And when we do turn to Him, He may stop the rain, shelter us from the worst of it, or remain with us as it pours: His concern is not our comfort, but our growth.

Perhaps clouds are forming in your life, or maybe the downpour has begun. Maybe you've been working to build your own shelter from the storm, and those efforts have proven futile. Whatever your situation, invite the Master Gardener to use this season to revive your spirit, grow your character, or renew

your strength in unexpected ways. And when the rain subsides, you'll appreciate even more the brightness of the sunshine.

*Lord, I ask for opportunities to grow closer to You. Should
they come in the form of a rainy day or rainy season, open my
heart so that I will know, without a doubt, that You are with me.
Open my eyes to see how You are growing me in ways I could
never have grown otherwise. Help me understand that rainy
days are just as essential as sunny ones to my growth in You.*

DROUGHT

The birds brought Elijah bread and meat every morning and
evening, and he drank water from the stream.

1 KINGS 17:6 NCV

Drought is one of a gardener's worst enemies. Unlike far too many people in the world, however, we first-world residents are blessed to have a water supply to draw from even when the rain doesn't fall. For much of history that wasn't the case.

Dubbed by King Ahab "the biggest troublemaker in Israel" (18:17 NCV), the prophet Elijah had stopped the rain. Actually, God stopped it in answer to Elijah's prayer, but the Israelites didn't turn to God despite their thirst. Unable to farm much, water their animals, or satisfy their own thirst, the Israelites were forced to make their search for water a daily priority.

Imagine how many trips to the well the Israelites made each day, how many wells dried up, and how many people, animals, and crops perished, yet God's people did not turn to Him. At this point, generations of Israelites had worshipped Baal and ignored multiple warnings from prophets to turn back to the God of Israel (1 Kings 12; 14; 16). Maybe now they thought Elijah's God wasn't real, didn't care, or wasn't powerful enough. And maybe you sometimes have similar thoughts.

Our minds, bodies, and spirits cannot hydrate themselves. So when our spirits are parched, do we pursue our other gods, as the Israelites did? Or do we sense the Holy Spirit's conviction and turn to Him for help? God gives us the freedom to choose. We can bury ourselves in busy-ness—or cry out to Him for help. We can take our frustrations out on someone else—or hit the pause button for rest and reflection.

God will use whatever it takes—removing our resources, blocking our escape hatches, and even drying out our water supply—to reach us. Whether you are among the faithful, the parched, or the proud, turn to your good and gracious God. He is ready to rain His blessings upon you.

Lord, my spirit is dry and my heart is brittle, for I
have dismissed Your generous offer of living water.
I have realized, though, that I can't control my life, I
don't have the answers I need, and I don't even know
how to seek them. I only know to turn to You.

HONEYBEES

*Be sure to fear the L*ORD *and serve him faithfully with all your*
heart; consider what great things he has done for you.

We may swat them, fear them, or ignore them, but honeybees are among the gardener's best friends.

Honeybees live in a highly structured, purposeful manner: each bee knows its role and fulfills it, strengthening the entire hive in the process. Honeybees travel great distances for food (sometimes up to six miles), support and assist the queen, and help build a strong shelter for everyone. And the entire time all this activity is happening, the world outside the hive is benefiting from their work.

You see, the United States alone spends billions of dollars on plants that honeybees are responsible for pollinating, and there simply is no substitute for their task. Whether they are pollinating tomatoes or potatoes, clover or flowers, honeybees are necessary to our ecosystem's very survival.

Likewise, when we serve—in our churches, schools, and communities—we may see ourselves as worker bees as opposed to the queen bee, but today's verse raises an important point for worker bees to consider. When we serve, are we willing to serve no matter how menial the task? Are we eager to serve, organized and proactively thinking ahead, or do we serve only if we have time? Are we willing to complete a job, or do we stop when our assignment gets challenging? The real issue is this: Do we serve the Lord with all our hearts?

Before you swat at or run from the next honeybee you see, consider first how hard it is working—for the hive, for the world, and for you. Then think about what you can learn from its example. And thank God for this reminder.

Thank You, God, for giving us a role model in the honeybee!
Help me be as industrious as it is, as committed to my
assigned task, and as responsible about completing
that task. No matter what my role is at a given time,
may I glorify You in all that I think, speak, and do.

PESTICIDES

Whoever dwells in the shelter of the Most High
will rest in the shadow of the Almighty.
I will say of the LORD, "He is my refuge and my fortress,
my God, in whom I trust."

Surely he will save you
from the fowler's snare
and from the deadly pestilence.

PSALM 91:1–3

D id you know that one of the best garden pesticides comes directly from God's own creation? A simple mixture of garlic and hot pepper steeped in water yields the safest, most effective pesticide for vegetables and other plants. Key to its effectiveness, however, is regular application; using it one time will not yield the same results as regular use will.

Today's verse emphasizes the significance of God's protection when we spend time with Him on a regular basis, when we abide in Him, when, so to speak, our approach is repeated application. The verbs *dwell, rest, trust,* and *save* suggest protection and peace. The nouns *shelter, fortress,* and *refuge* indicate a permanent structure, a place that will not change or move. And the phrases *fowler's snare* and *deadly pestilence* powerfully reveal why we need God's almighty protection.

After all, the fowler—Satan himself—is ever-present, conniving and scheming, working to create snares that hurt us and lead us away from God. Whether Satan is throwing temptation at our doorstep, luring us toward a godless path, distracting us with his lies, or hitting us with a debilitating illness, God is with us. And when our daily habit is to stay close to God—to read His Word, dwell in His presence, and rest in His shadow—the enemy's power is thwarted. No matter what difficulty we find ourselves in, we have God's promise of constant protection and secure salvation.

So in this sin-marred creation, a healthy plant gets attacked by leaf-eating bugs or disease, yet with regular treatment, that plant will survive and even thrive. In this sin-marred creation, we experience spiritual attacks, yet God protects us from physical as well as spiritual destruction. And how glorious to know, without a doubt, that we can find rest in the shelter of the Almighty.

Father God, I am grateful to know that You are with me, always acting to keep me safe both physically and spiritually. I find peace in the fact that You are greater than any of the enemy's schemes. Thank You for the assurance of Your power and the knowledge that I can walk through my days protected by You.

NATURAL PESTICIDE RECIPE

Mix 3 Tbsp hot pepper flakes (or 10 fresh hot peppers, minced) and four cloves minced garlic with two cups of water. Let the mixture steep for twenty-four hours. (You may want to do this outside because the smell is *not* pleasant.) Strain the mixture and add a half-gallon of water. Spray primarily on leaves with regular application, and no worries if some gets on fruits or vegetables, the flavor won't be affected.

LIVING AMONG WEEDS

"Let both [the wheat and the tares] grow together until the harvest, and at the time of harvest I will say to the reapers, 'First gather together the tares and bind them in bundles to burn them, but gather the wheat into my barn.'"

Jesus in Matthew 13:30 NKJV

We pull them, spray them, ignore them, and ultimately realize that we're fighting a losing battle because weeds will always be with us.

But as counterintuitive as this sounds, weeds can be a good thing. That's right! Weeds can tell us a lot about unhealthy soil conditions. Clover, for example, might indicate that soil is low in nitrogen; buttercups might indicate poor drainage; flowering weeds like chickweed may actually reveal the best place to grow certain fruits and vegetables. Still, whatever the reasons for weed growth, it's often better to let them grow a bit before pulling them.

For one thing, when the growth is just a sprout, we can't always distinguish a weed from a cultivated plant. How often have we pulled weeds only to discover they were early shoots of plants we wanted in our garden! Furthermore, young plants might be disturbed by weed pulling: not yet mature, they don't have a strong enough root system to withstand a nearby weed being yanked from the ground. Finally, some weeds actually help strengthen a plant's chances of survival: many types of weeds have root systems that allow air and nutrients to enter the soil.

According to today's Scripture, God allows believers and unbelievers to "grow together." Notice that Jesus didn't say that these metaphorical weeds should be pulled as early as possible.

One reason is that our personal prejudices and judgments may at first hinder us from clearly and accurately seeing a person's sincerity. It takes time to get a sense of the integrity of someone's beliefs, especially if that person is reserved or if we have preconceived notions because of his appearance or her background. Or we may meet people who say and do all the right things, but after we observe them in the daily trenches of life, we see that their actions are inconsistent and their faith doesn't seem as strong as we first thought. Put differently, we may have thought they were fruit-producing plants, but it becomes evident they are weeds.

Bottom line, the presence of weeds can indicate cracks in a church's spiritual foundation. Some unhealthy conditions or unbiblical attitudes may need to be addressed before real growth can occur within that church body. Whether within the four walls of church or the four corners of a garden, we need to be mindful of weeds and how best to deal with them.

Father God, guide me in my weeding of the garden of my life. I want to be wise: I want to get rid of anything that would impair my growth in You.

WIND

We live by faith, not by sight.

2 CORINTHIANS 5:7

Unless it's whipped up into a frenzy, we hardly notice the wind. Yet without it, the world would be very different, and many kinds of life would struggle to survive. After all, wind moves weather systems, and breezes carry seeds, pollen, water, and a constant supply of oxygen. Wind is a force that we do not see; we only see and feel its effects.

Similarly, we do not see the great force of our great God as we walk through our days, but everywhere we look we see and feel the effects of His presence with us, His goodness, His generosity, His love, and His grace. Rather than only checking in with God about big issues in our day, may we live with our eyes and heart wide open to seeing and celebrating evidence of His goodness and love. Here's a handful of ideas to help you start seeing more clearly evidence of God in your world:

- If you're reading this, you woke up this morning. That means you're breathing.
- If you can read this, that means someone taught you to read. That means you received an education.
- If you are reading this at the breakfast table, you have food to eat. And a home.
- If you are reading this in your work space, you have income.
- If you found time to read this, you had at least a few minutes to yourself.

This list could go on, but the point is that even when we don't see God, we can see evidence of His presence and experience the blessed effects of that presence. May we never overlook the Provider of these blessings, big and small.

Pause for just a moment today to notice the wind—or at least evidence of its presence. Pause, too, to take a spiritual breath of the Holy Spirit. Thank Him for the love, joy, peace, patience, kindness, goodness, faithfulness, gentleness, and self-control He brings into your life.

Lord, forgive me for taking for granted Your presence in my heart and in my life. Help me have eyes that see You in all I do today. And thank You for Your faithfulness to me even when I've not been mindful of You.

NOTHING IS MAINTENANCE-FREE

Those false teachers are like springs without water and clouds blown by a storm. A place in the blackest darkness has been kept for them. They brag with words that mean nothing. By their evil desires they lead people into the trap of sin—people who are just beginning to escape from others who live in error.

2 Peter 2:17–18 NCV

Rose lovers should have known it was too good to be true. We shouldn't have let our guard down . . .

A while back Knock Out roses were all the rage—and why not? They were billed as maintenance-free! No pruning, no upkeep, and resistant to black spot disease. But this ease of care made for less attentive gardeners, and the deadly virus rose rosette found its way into Knock Outs, producing bright red shoots and distorted blooms. Spread by mites, rose rosette is difficult to get rid of, so it managed to spread unchecked, in large part because Knock Outs were allegedly maintenance-free. Gardeners weren't paying attention.

Knock Out roses remind me of the "gospels" being presented as truth today. These uplifting messages presented without scriptural support and sermons promoting name-it/claim-it "faith" are dangerously popular. The messengers can fill football stadiums with their misguided gospels and relative "truths."

All too often these teachers are left unchecked and allowed to spread their messages because biblically literate believers have not challenged them with God's truth. We have basically allowed some pastors and teachers to become maintenance-free. We don't check for viruses of untruth or disease-bearing mites. Knock Outs suffered when gardeners left these supposedly maintenance-free roses alone. Similarly, new or naïve believers suffer when more mature Christians leave unbiblical teachers alone.

Ask the Holy Spirit to help you filter the teachings of those you listen to. Dig deeply into God's Word to be certain of what it says—and able to identify untruths when you hear them. False teachers are not going away, but God provides His Word and His ever-present Counselor to help us avoid their infection—no matter how appealing their message or pretty the packaging may be.

*Holy Spirit, I ask You to give me wisdom and discernment
as I listen to my teachers—in church, in the media, in
books, in articles friends send me. Enable me to know with
certainty whether or not the lessons are Your truth.*

ZINNIAS

Though you have not seen [Jesus], you love him; and even though you do not see him now, you believe in him and are filled with an inexpressible and glorious joy.

1 Peter 1:8

While none of us can adequately explain why, the response to zinnias is fairly universal: no one can look upon a patch of them without smiling! Bright punches of color, uncomplicated yet beautiful blooms, their little necks straining upward to the sun, zinnias can turn around a bad mood quickly. We look at them and smile—and some gardeners insist that zinnias smile right back at them.

Peter wrote of another reason to smile, that being "an inexpressible and glorious joy" resulting from our love of—and faith in—Someone we have never seen. Joy is different from happiness, the latter being dependent on temporary circumstances and the former, on eternal reasons to celebrate. Think about a time when, despite your situation, you were surprised by a bit of joy. Maybe you were dealing with a lingering crisis, hit with shocking news, or sleepwalking through a season of confusion . . . when suddenly you noticed in your heart a deep, abiding joy that brought peace and said, "All is well." In those heaven-sent moments, we aren't denying reality and dismissing our trials. Instead, by God's grace, we are experiencing the joy that results when we connect with the One who is the Source of deep, lasting, unshakable hope. With the new opportunities of each day, we can choose to overanalyze or even dismiss the Lord's gift of joy. Or, like our response to the zinnias, we can with gratitude accept His simple gift of beauty, knowing we have caught a glimpse of what is real and true.

God's love, His grace, and His joy come to us in many forms, one of them being in the simple yet delightful zinnia that naturally spreads its cheer. Plant a patch of zinnias and let them remind you of that inexplicable joy the Lord blesses His children with. Savor those moments and receive them as His reminder to you that all is well.

Precious Lord, I have never seen You with my eyes, but I love You. And I thank You, Lord, for the peace and joy You pour into my heart. May Your presence in my life spark the kind of smiles that Your zinnias do.

WATERSHEDS

Have mercy upon me, O God,
According to Your lovingkindness;
According to the multitude of Your tender mercies,
Blot out my transgressions.
Wash me thoroughly from my iniquity,
And cleanse me from my sin.

PSALM 51:1–2 NKJV

G ardeners and non-gardeners alike have experienced spiritual watershed moments, those turning points in life that make a huge difference in who we are and where we're headed. Christians live with an awareness of the ultimate watershed moment for every human being, that moment of facing the holy God.

Gardeners, however, also understand physical watersheds—those geographical areas that include rivers and streams as well as the lakes they flow into—and gardeners know very well why even non-gardeners should care about watersheds. You see, the water in a watershed is untreated: chemical and organic pollutants prevent this water from being used for drinking, recreation (swimming, fishing), and irrigating crops. "Adopt a Watershed" initiatives encourage communities to make a few adjustments that will dramatically improve their area's water supply. Rain gardens, recycling, and picking up after pets are just a few simple ways people can help keep their local watershed clean.

Like water flowing through the watershed to its ultimate destination of a pond or lake, you and I flow through this life picking up pollutants, becoming both less and less useful to God and less and less appealing to those around us. Then all of us flow through life to the spiritual watershed moment when we stand before the Almighty. As believers, our hope is in the Living Water, in Jesus who has washed us clean from the pollutant of sin and thereby made us a source of life for people both inside and outside of His family.

When the apostle Paul wrote in Galatians 6:2 that we are to help one another with our "troubles," (NCV) he was talking about our sin, but in other parts of the New Testament, Paul included all of life's burdens and trials. If we are to know God's pleasure in us at the ultimate watershed moment of life, we are to encourage, support, and comfort one another.

So ask God to give you the name of someone who could use a friend today—and if you yourself need a friend, reach out to someone you know and trust. Let your ultimate Friend love and encourage you through that person.

Gracious Father, thank You for providing me the Living Water of Your Son—for water that cleanses me, quenches my thirst, and enables me to grow in my knowledge of and love for You! Show me today, I ask, who needs a drink and/or who might be willing to give me a drink.

GOD'S GREENHOUSE

You, O Lord, will bless the righteous;
With favor You will surround him as with a shield.

PSALM 5:12 NKJV

Whatever their size, shape, and special features, all greenhouses are intended to protect plants from harsh conditions they would not naturally be able to withstand. A greenhouse, for instance, can be an ideal place to start seeds, grow tropical plants, and preserve transplants. What a sweet deal for those chosen plants!

We who know Jesus as Savior and Lord also have a place of protection from harsh conditions we would not naturally be able to withstand on our own. That place is the shield of God's protective presence. He is surrounding us so that we can grow in conditions we could not otherwise withstand. And in ways only God understands, rather than confine us, the shield of His constant presence actually makes us truly free—free to grow, try new experiences, and meet new people without fear. Even if we stumble or when we face temptation, we have God's Holy Spirit with us, protecting us in whatever way He deems best.

That is a wonderful truth, isn't it? We can trust that God is with us. This doesn't mean we won't encounter trouble or have a pain-free life; but no person, situation, loss, pain, or disease, and not even death itself will undo our sure salvation in Him.

So how will God's greenhouse protection manifest itself in your life today? Will you be free of fear? Will you trust Him with the climate controls? Will you take a divinely guided step of faith and trust in God's promised protection?

Precious Father, I have been reluctant to
_____ because of my fear of
_____. I confess this as a lack of trust
in Your promise to protect me. May Your Spirit overwhelm
me with courage and enable me to blaze a new trail—one
that You map out for me—in my day, my week, my year,
my life. I thank You for the shield of Your protection.

PERMACULTURE

The LORD God put the man in the garden of Eden to care for it and work it.

GENESIS 2:15 NCV

Maybe you've heard the gardening buzzword *permaculture*—but do you know what it means? Merriam-Webster defines it as "an agricultural system or method that seeks to integrate human activity with natural surroundings so as to create highly efficient self-sustaining ecosystems." The ethics that stem from this perspective—the ethics of caring for the planet and sharing with fellow inhabitants—can impact every aspect of our lives, from health, to finances, to technology, to food, to gardening, and beyond.

In gardening, for instance, the acts of composting, recycling materials and supplies, companion planting, sharing surplus, and seed saving/storage are a few ways permaculture principles are applied to daily life. Permaculture does not claim Christian roots, but it definitely sets forth biblical values. After all, when did it become okay for Christians to stop caring about or caring for God's creation—the earth, the animals, the people? How did some of us come to deem ecological responsibility an untouchable political issue or a fiscally irresponsible concern? When did it become acceptable for us to neglect the poor or disregard the elderly?

Instead, may we love the planet God created and its people as an act of heartfelt worship, gratitude to our Provider, and respect for all He has made. Each one of us can choose—each one of us can learn—to live like this. Oh, we'll need the heart of Christ, and He will indeed empower us to live a life that glorifies Him: a life of worship, gratitude, and care for His creation.

Creator God, give me Your eyes and Your heart to see something I can do to clean up or protect the world You crafted. Maybe I make use of that dusty recycling bin, work in a community garden, or share my garden's surplus. Whatever you call me to be busy about, keep my eyes fixed on You, the Creator of the ultimate permaculture.

NOAH'S VINEYARD

*"Everything that lives and moves about will be food for you. Just as
I gave you the green plants, I now give you everything."... Noah, a
man of the soil, proceeded to plant a vineyard. When he drank some
of its wine, he became drunk and lay uncovered inside his tent.*

GENESIS 9:3, 20–21

He endured ridicule, he witnessed all of creation destroyed, and he survived.

Noah had firsthand knowledge of God's power and strength; Noah knew that the only reason he, his family, and the animals on the ark survived was because of his choice to obey God and by God's great faithfulness when he did so. And God had gifted Noah and his family with a new world.

What a picture of the kind of relationship God longs to have with His people! We see Noah's trust, obedience, perseverance, and hope as well as the Almighty's faithfulness and provision. Against this glorious background, the account of Noah's vineyard seems a rather odd story to include. Noah planted a vineyard showing that he intended to work and care for the land as God intended him to. So why this misstep? As with all of God's Word, it was to teach us an important and relevant lesson.

And the lesson—the word of warning to us—is this: Noah was sidetracked by the fruit of his labor, and his actions were shameful. Similarly, when we boast of our possessions, when we brag about a child's winning project that we actually did ourselves, when we laud our many accomplishments—however inflated—to someone so that person will know how fabulous we are, when we negotiate a financial arrangement that will certainly cheat another, when we

misuse the gifts God entrusts to us, we are just as drunk on our ego and pride—
we are just as naked and vulnerable—as Noah was drunk on wine. Clearly, the
flood did not wipe out sin from the world; it wasn't time yet. But Jesus' death
on the cross has provided us a way to conquer it.

Noah was "a man of the soil" who planted a vineyard. He knew how to
farm, and he used his skills. But then Noah kept too much of the vineyard's
success for himself. What are you planting today—and for whose glory?

*Lord, You have entrusted certain skills and gifts
to me. Show me where I am using them to bring
glory to me rather than to glorify You.*

HEIRLOOM PLANTS

Tell your children about [the land laid to waste],
Let your children tell their children,
And their children another generation.

JOEL 1:3 NKJV

Some heirloom plants have been passed down for hundreds of years, and the reasons are as diverse as the plants themselves: better flavor, better texture, sentimental value, no genetic modifications, etc. By and large, though, these heirlooms do not grow well in commercial gardens because they are usually quite temperamental. They need loving, individualized care and handling, and they must be harvested by hand.

The prophet Joel spoke of another type of heirloom—a spiritual one. We don't have much information about this man of God, but we do have the message God spoke through him, urging the elders of Judah to pass down God's lessons to the younger generations. The people had grown complacent about sin and its consequences. As a result, accounts of important experiences as well as crucial truths about God were slipping further away with each generation.

Warning the people that God's patience would eventually end, Joel compared the results of the coming destruction to a crop devoured by an army of locusts. The people would find themselves at a point where revival would no longer be possible. Joel called the people to turn back to God, so that neither they nor future generations would suffer.

Joel's message, however, is not all doom and gloom; he does offer hope for those people who repent of their sin and appeal to God's mercy. Today, we find that hope in Jesus—but will the next generation? Only if we pass along this most important heirloom: the gospel message, coupled with our testimony of God's faithfulness to us personally. We can hope they learn from our mistakes, accept biblical counsel, and build their lives on the foundation of God's truth and His values. Just like growing those heirloom plants, this process requires loving, individualized care and handling.

And nothing fuels our efforts to reach the next generation with this heirloom message like our own passion for God. Ask Him to enable you to share effectively the precious spiritual heirlooms that will edify the hearts and minds of the next generation.

Father God, I long to build a spiritual legacy that honors You by pointing to You. Enable me to boldly pass along my spiritual treasures to those who will journey behind me.

WHEN ROOTS GO HAYWIRE

They are like well-watered plants in the sunshine
that spread their roots all through the garden.
They wrap their roots around a pile of rocks
and look for a place among the stones.

JOB 8:16–17 NCV

Job's "friend" Bildad spoke these words about "those who forget God" (v. 13), suggesting that Job was suffering because he had put his faith and trust in something other than the one true God of Israel. Although Bildad's diagnosis of Job's predicament was totally incorrect, his words offer insight and truth for both literal and figurative gardeners.

When a plant is well-watered and receives life-giving sunlight, it will grow and flourish. Above the ground we see fresh leaves, perhaps a bloom, or fruit, but most of a plant's growth happens below the earth's surface. And the part we don't see can either benefit or wreak havoc on the plant.

Bildad described the plant as spreading its roots, looking everywhere for nourishment. A plant's roots can indeed go haywire. Sometimes, even when every need has been met, roots search for nourishment in all the wrong places. This misguided search results in roots wrapping themselves around rocks and stones, "thinking" that at some point the right rock will give them what they need. But that right rock is never found. After all, apart from God's divine intervention, what rock can nourish a plant?

Even if a plant looks good on the surface, its roots can get tired and dry up when they cling tightly to what cannot nourish them. Similarly, our fervent search for the next thrill, the next big thing, the next word of affirmation will make us tired and dry up our soul. The pursuit of God Himself is the only quest that gives life. We should not cling to anything else.

So right now throw some stones. Release them. In fact, release into God's care your shortened breath, your tense muscles, your sleepless nights, your edgy temperament, all the things above the surface as well as the stones you've been collecting below the surface and are clinging to.

Lord, as I breathe, let me inhale Your goodness and exhale my worries and my stress. Thank You that, as I stop clinging to things not of You, You take those burdens and fill me with Your love and grace.

TOMATO DISORDERS

Forgive and comfort him [who has caused grief], so that
he will not be overwhelmed by excessive sorrow.

2 CORINTHIANS 2:7

Tomatoes are susceptible to four common disorders: cat face, sunscald, cracking, and blossom-end rot. And disorders are different from diseases because in most cases, fruit with disorders may still be eaten. While a commercial grower deems fruit unmarketable because of the altered appearance, backyard farmers don't hesitate to enjoy the less-than-picture-perfect tomatoes from their garden. After all, unless a tomato remains on the vine too long, disorders usually don't affect its flavor or nutritional value. Gardeners also know that when the affected portion is cut off, what's left may be consumed without worry. The tomato won't look as good, but it is certainly worth salvaging for a chopped salad, salsa, or sauce.

Why do we not handle our precious relationships the same way gardeners handle their homegrown tomatoes? When someone has wronged us, we tend to be like that commercial grower: we throw out the entire relationship. Or we may let the wrong remain on the vine too long and find ourselves building up so much bitterness and resentment that the relationship seems beyond salvaging. Instead of any of these options, why don't we—like the tomato gardener—assess the relationship's value and, if we consider it worth salvaging, remove the affected portion in order to save it?

Remember, disorders are not the same as diseases. So we need to be careful not to confuse a relationship that has hit a bump in the road with one that's unhealthy, toxic, or abusive. Let's also do our part to remedy relationships by practicing forgiveness. Forgiving someone who has hurt us is not only blessed obedience, but it also frees us from the burden of bitterness. As for the relationship, it may never look the same, but in whatever ways it is different, that relationship just might be more life-giving than ever.

Father God, I have been struggling to forgive
_____because of _____. Please
give me wisdom to discern the true value of our relationship,
give me power over my own pride to forgive, and help me to
do what I can to restore what the enemy has tried to destroy.

UNFAILING WATERS

If you extend your soul to the hungry
And satisfy the afflicted soul,
Then your light shall dawn in the darkness,
And your darkness shall be as the noonday.
The LORD will guide you continually,
And satisfy your soul in drought,
And strengthen your bones;
You shall be like a watered garden,
And like a spring of water, whose waters do not fail.

ISAIAH 58:10–11 NKJV

Can you imagine never having to water your garden again? On the flip side, what if you had a spring "whose waters do not fail" to keep your plants hydrated according to their individual needs?

We are assured of this perpetual watering of our souls when we both receive the love and grace God gives us through Christ and extend it to the poor, the afflicted, the sorrowful. When we do so, our souls will never thirst. The Lord promises that He will keep our souls and hearts refreshed, and we simply cannot outgive Him.

So could your soul use some satisfaction? Does your heart need refreshment? Look around and see who needs love. Who among you needs care? Or justice? Or mercy? Or food, clothing, or shelter? Meditate on the words of Isaiah and recall the example of servanthood that Jesus Himself is for us. Then let God use you to be a light that points the people around you to the One who sent you, the One whose waters "do not fail."

Lord, show me the person whose path I cross today who needs my help, who needs a touch of Your love this day. Then enable me to love with Your generous love, to serve with Your selflessness, and, if the opportunity arises, to speak the gospel truth in love. And what a blessing to know that as I follow Your example in this way, You will refresh my soul.

OVERWATERING

"You are the light of the world."

JESUS IN MATTHEW 5:14

It may seem odd or even inconceivable, but a plant can actually have too much water. A plant can have too much of a good and life-giving thing! When they're overwatered, plants yellow and then die.

Can we as followers of Christ be overwatered? Can we have too much of a good Christian thing and somehow become less useful to God? Oliver Wendell Holmes Sr. once observed, "Some people are so heavenly minded that they are no earthly good." Whether or not you totally agree, this statement offers a good word of warning.

But just what are some good things that we may get too much of to the detriment of our usefulness on this earth? Christian fellowship is a vital good for our faith walk, but "too much Christian fellowship" can mean isolation from people who don't yet know about God's love for them.

Christian literature offers wonderful truths in memorable and even life-changing ways. But too much of this good may result in less time spent reading God's Word and learning His truth for ourselves.

All believers need water, but oversaturation can indeed mean a stunt of growth in our faith.

Lord God, I don't want to be so heavenly minded that
I'm no earthly good to You or to the people around me.
Guide my use of time so that my life is in balance and
so that You can use me as light in this dark world.

STAKING

Bear one another's burdens, and so fulfill the law of Christ.

GALATIANS 6:2 ESV

Some plants—like tomatoes, peppers, eggplant, hollyhocks, delphiniums, gladiolus—need extra support in order to thrive. Their flowers or fruits are usually too heavy for the plant to support, and sometimes that fruit could rot if it touches the soil or scald if not protected by foliage.

The solution to this is staking. A branch, a length of bamboo, or even a store-bought stake will work. Gardeners simply take a thin strip of cloth and, at intervals, tie the plant to the stake. Whatever staking system is used, the function is the same: provide extra support to the plant when its blooms and fruit are more than the plant itself can bear.

Sometimes we try to support more people and problems than we can bear on our own. The burdens of life can seem impossible for us to manage. And that's when we can take the idea of staking out of the garden into our friendships: we can be the stake for the woman whose child was arrested for drugs, whose husband was unfaithful to her, or who was just diagnosed with cancer. Whatever the burden, if a woman we know is allowed to remain "down," she risks rotting away in depression and loneliness, but if her situation is too exposed, she could get burned by gossip and assumption.

When we offer our time, our listening ear, and our prayers, we can support these hurting women whom God loves the same way that a stake supports a plant in the garden. When we willingly bind ourselves to this person for her sake, her burdens will no longer be as heavy. In fact, those burdens become purposeful—refining character, strengthening faith, and eventually providing an avenue of ministry to someone walking a similar path.

Who in your world needs staking today? Reach out to her; invite her to join you for coffee or lunch. And ask the Lord to equip you to be a strong stake for this person whose burdens are heavy.

> *Lord Jesus, my heart aches for _____, and I don't know how best to support her. Help me reach out to her with the love and grace You have shown me—and help her to know she has a trusted friend in me and especially in You.*

BLIGHT AND POWDERY MILDEW

"I blasted you with blight and mildew.
When your gardens increased,
Your vineyards,
Your fig trees,
And your olive trees,
The locust devoured them;
Yet you have not returned to Me,"
Says the LORD.

AMOS 4:9 NKJV

Two common problems vegetable growers face are blight and powdery mildew. Blight results from a pathogen, a host, and a lot of rain, and powdery mildew—unlike other mildews—appears without any moisture present. Both blight and powdery mildew can sneak up on an unsuspecting gardener and damage a crop. Blight will eventually kill a plant; powdery mildew will make a plant unsightly. The fruit produced by plants affected by either will have compromised flavor. Plants affected by either will not produce fruit that anyone would want to buy.

And God sent locusts as well as both blight and mildew to attack Israel's abundant crops. Because of the nature of the two diseases, farmers in that time could do nothing to rescue their crops. In attacking the Israelites' food supply, God impacted their economy and their health, yet the people ignored His warnings. God then confronted Israel about their behavior, admonishing them for their arrogant boasting and lack of concern for the poor, telling them that they must now face Him and that He would hold them accountable for their actions.

At some point we will face Him too. Each one of us. Thankfully and by God's grace, we have a Savior who died in our place as punishment for our sin, but we will still need to account for what we do or don't do for our Lord during our time on this earth. Have you pushed aside and tried to ignore something the Lord has laid upon your heart to do? Maybe it's something simple like calling a friend or taking a meal to a family going through hard times. Or maybe that something is bigger, like a new ministry or a change of vocation. Take some time today to be quiet and listen expectantly for God's quiet voice. Do this regularly until you know what He would have you do and when. The kind of fruit you bear as a result of obedience will bless others and glorify God.

Lord, have I been too busy to listen for Your voice? Clear my mind of anxieties and responsibilities. I open to You my heart, my head, and my spirit. Direct my hands, my feet, my words, and my ears so that I may please You today.

COMPOSTING

*"Unless a grain of wheat falls into the ground and dies, it remains alone;
but if it dies, it produces much grain. He who loves his life will lose it,
and he who hates his life in this world will keep it for eternal life."*

JESUS IN JOHN 12:24–25 NKJV

What do you do with your lawn clippings and table scraps? Or even the items that have lingered in the pantry or refrigerator a bit too long? Rather than discarding them, many gardeners and environmentalists make compost.

Compost is, essentially, broken-down organic matter made from fruits and vegetables that are no longer edible, peelings, rinds, and the like. Barrels, piles, bins, even cones are all viable containers to use when making compost. Whatever you choose, the technique, the list of dos and don'ts, and the goals are the same: composters want a product that will fortify the soil and thereby stimulate healthy growth in plants and crops. The heat generated from the compost pile refines our garbage into something fertile, something that edifies, to spread among our gardens.

In the same way, Christ took our sin to the grave, transforming our decay into life—a gift He intends His followers to receive, share, and spread throughout the world. Depending on the state of our heart, the process will vary—our "breaking down" and the decomposition of our sin will take different amounts of time—but when the process is complete, we will be fortified to share our experience so that others may know of the same transforming grace.

Whether you purchase compost or make your own, take a moment to consider its humble beginnings. At one point it was waste; now, transformed, it offers nourishment, growth, and—for the gardener—hope. Think about how your own spiritual journey from sin to hope has fed your soul, revived your spirit, and grown your faith in Jesus. Right now, whether you are in a refining fire, easily sharing your joy, or struggling to overcome a particular sin, thank God for His power at work in your life.

Lord Jesus, I cannot fathom why You took on my sin, but I am grateful that You did. Thank You for transforming me, for rescuing me from a sinful state of decay and giving me new life. May I freely share about Your grace and power with others so that they, too, can experience renewal and growth in You.

PULLING WEEDS

You have heard about my past life in the Jewish religion. I attacked the church of God and tried to destroy it. . . . But God had special plans for me and set me apart for his work even before I was born. He called me through his grace.

GALATIANS 1:13, 15 NCV

Have you heard about Paul's past life? He was committed to the Jewish faith, confident of its truth, and openly persecuting the followers of this rabbi from Galilee who taught a different Way of salvation. Clearly, Paul's was a heart that—like yours and mine—needed some weeds pulled out. Jesus surprised Paul when He showed up to do that weeding Himself.

Humbling does not even begin to describe what happened to Paul on the road to Damascus. God charged him to preach the gospel of Christ to non-Jews, but first Paul had to do some explaining to the Jewish Christians. Was his change of heart genuine?

Paul realized that he had to stop what he had been doing. Weeds had grown tall and thick in his heart. They wouldn't fade away with a chemical spray. Those weeds were too established to be choked out by new seeds sown among them. There was only one effective approach: Paul had to reach down deep, get his hands dirty, and yank out those weeds from root to tip. No weeds and no part of a weed could remain, because Paul could not do the Lord's work without a clean heart. And neither can we.

In both the garden and our hearts, pulling weeds is tedious, painful, and absolutely essential: it clears the way for healthy growth. A weed-free heart enables us to serve wherever and whenever God calls us to serve.

Take some time today to do some weeding—and then commit to stay on top of it!

> *Holy Spirit, help me see the weeds in my heart and then enable me to uproot them completely. Then, I pray, plant in me Your goodness and love, so that I may do the work God set apart for me to do.*

UNTAPPED HARVEST

[Jesus] said to his disciples, "The harvest is plentiful but the workers are few. Ask the Lord of the harvest, therefore, to send out workers into his harvest field."

MATTHEW 9:37–38

I f you've ever stumbled upon a patch of wild blackberries, it is a wondrous gift! Somehow this untended patch brings forth sweet fruit: clearly the soil is fertile enough and conditions favorable enough to produce berries. And when you discover this little corner of the world, you experience the joy of harvesting without having done any work at all! And that was exactly the message Jesus wanted His disciples to understand. . . .

Many people we know are searching and searching. They have acknowledged that material wealth isn't making them happy, and they know that cycling through relationships and marriages isn't satisfying. But they haven't yet figured out specifically what—or for whom—they are looking. We know they are searching for Jesus, but they don't know that. Yet.

Now harvesting wild blackberries is different from harvesting potatoes, basil, or tomatoes. Some of us will have more success with basil than potatoes, while another may do better with potatoes than tomatoes. While you read these thoughts, a person who fits Jesus' description may have come to mind. But you may be thinking, *Oh no! I know she seems lost and is searching for truth, but I don't think I could ever go there with her.* Ask the Holy Spirit to guide you and equip you—and remember that while your words may sound stumbly-jumbly to you, they may sound as sweet as music to her. The Holy Spirit sees to that!

Maybe, though, you're not sure what harvest field the Lord has for you. If that's the case, ask Him to direct you to it. No matter which type of field you will be harvesting—and that field may end up being closer than you expected—remember that the Gardener has already planted the seed and cultivated it. Your role is to harvest. And like the tasty fruit from that unexpected patch of wild blackberries, the rewards of working in the Lord's harvest are sweet and satisfying.

Holy Spirit, thank You for allowing me to be a part of God's work. Guide me to where I can harvest fruit for His eternal kingdom—and equip me to do so properly.

CALL OF THE WILD

"Consider how the wild flowers grow. They do not labor or spin. Yet I tell you, not even Solomon in all his splendor was dressed like one of these. If that is how God clothes the grass of the field, which is here today, and tomorrow is thrown into the fire, how much more will he clothe you—you of little faith!"

JESUS IN LUKE 12:27–28

Walk in a forest, through a meadow, or even along a mountain trail, and you'll find different elements of nature's garden at their best. You'll find grasses, flowers, trees, and maybe even a twisted tangle of wild blackberries or raspberries hidden in a thicket. These wild, unkempt gardens are in stark contrast to the perfectly manicured, well-planned lawns and gardens we see in established neighborhoods. Nature's gardens are not uniform and trimmed the way our gardens are, but they truly have a beauty all their own.

No human cares for these plants. No landscaper or gardener comes in to edge, fertilize, thin, or prune. No greenhouse protects them during inclement weather. We're not often aware of what dies, but we can see and enjoy all that survives. And much does survive and thrive as these plants rely solely on God's hand to feed and water them, to care for and provide for them, and to determine when it's time to leave the organic world. And what they leave behind nourishes what's yet to come. That cycle is part of God's plan for His creation.

In the same way, when we relinquish control of our lives and rely solely on God, we can be sure that many unexpected and untamed experiences will grow us in directions we had not planned or anticipated. Certain life events and experiences will challenge us, strengthen us, and maybe even defy social conventions, yet we can welcome them as God-given opportunities to leave a legacy for generations to come.

So, the next time you wander through a natural garden, consider that—like you—the plant's very survival depends solely on the same Creator that your survival depends on. And be assured that the Master Gardener's attention will never slack.

Heavenly Father, when I consider the beautiful plants of untamed nature, I am reminded of all the ways You care for me—and I can't help but wonder about those times that I have been and that I still am unaware of Your care. Thank You for Your faithfulness even when I am less than true to You.

THE SEASONS

"While the earth remains,
Seedtime and harvest,
Cold and heat,
Winter and summer,
And day and night
Shall not cease."

GENESIS 8:22 NKJV

Maybe it's just human nature, but have you noticed that we are rarely, if ever, satisfied with the weather? In the summer, we complain of the heat and, in some regions, the humidity; in the winter, we don't like the cold. When it rains, we long for sunny days; when we have weeks of sunshine, we complain about having to water our lawns and gardens. Each season means different responsibilities and different opportunities in our garden, yet we always seem to want the opposite of whatever we're receiving. What fickle creatures we are!

God knows very well that our hearts are fickle, yet He never stops pursuing us. Today's verse, for instance, is His promise that He will never destroy the earth again until Christ's return. That promise means that in this season of God's history, each one of us can return to Him, commune with Him, receive His blessings, and know His peace. What wonderful purposes! And the four seasons of the year—however they unfold in your area—are also purposeful: each one brings opportunities of its own.

So instead of complaining during one season because you long for the opposite season, let's receive each new season as God's beautiful reminder that

He is the God of opportunities. In fact, with each change of season, may we listen for what the Father wants to tell us about our spiritual season and the opportunities He has for us.

Precious Father, thank You for the seasons of my life that—like the seasons of the planting year—offer unique opportunities for my spiritual growth. And thank You, Master Gardener, for faithfully tending my soul. May I cooperate with You, that You may be glorified by the fruit my life yields.

BUTTERFLIES

If anyone is in Christ, he is a new creation; old things have
passed away; behold, all things have become new.

2 CORINTHIANS 5:17 NKJV

Rebirth can be a difficult concept to understand, but the lovely little butterfly offers a picture of what takes place when Christ comes into a human heart. The caterpillar's metamorphosis provides a wonderful illustration of a believer's spiritual transformation:

- The caterpillar or larva is in the feeding phase. It eats the leaves in its world just as we feed on the ideas of the world around us.
- At the chrysalis or pupa stage, the caterpillar appears lifeless. Jesus' lifeless body was taken down off the cross and placed in a tomb. A believer's chrysalis stage is when we die to sin.
- The caterpillar emerges from its cocoon, transformed into a completely new creature. Similarly, we who recognize our sin, confess it, receive God's forgiveness, and accept Jesus Christ as our Savior and Lord are transformed into new life in Him.

The butterfly does not return to the caterpillar state; nor can it return to the pupa phase. When a butterfly emerges from its cocoon, it flies—something it couldn't do before! The butterfly also drinks sweet nectar instead of gorging on leaves.

Are you a new creation in Christ still trying to gorge on leaves? If so, do you find them choking you? Are you a new creation in Christ still trying to crawl back inside the cocoon to live as you once lived? Even if you could go back in time, leaves would no longer nourish you, and the torn cocoon would no longer protect you. Why? Because God has transformed you into a new creation. Now you have the blessed privilege and opportunity to soar in His power and do His work on this planet. So spread your wings into their full, beautiful glory. It's time to fly.

Lord Jesus, at times I want to return to the cocoon, and at other times I want to gorge on the world's ideas and values. Thank You for the beautiful reminder of the butterfly that never turns back to an earlier stage of life. Thank You, too, for this lovely symbol of both Your resurrection and my transformation.

WAITING

If we hope for what we do not yet have, we wait for it patiently.

ROMANS 8:25

All of us who garden know that there is a hand-off point in the process: we have done all we can, and now nature must take its course. We can plan, prepare, and assist, but we can't hasten the growth of a vegetable. Coaxing, screaming, begging, pleading, demanding, negotiating—none of these tactics will bring a tomato to ripeness or cause a pepper to burst forth from its blossom. Scientists have developed shortcuts like genetic modifications and climate-controlled environments, but God's way is still the best for producing delicious flavor and significant nutritional value. So rather than looking for other shortcuts, we do our part . . . and then we wait. Patiently. After all, growth is a process that takes time. *Sigh* . . .

Are we as patient regarding prayers we offer the Lord? Do we wait patiently after we make a request? Do we ask sincerely for a change of heart when He helps us realize that our requests are not aligned with His will? Or do we coax, beg, try to negotiate, or even attempt to manipulate God rather than choosing patience and humility?

Patience does not come easily for many of us, but—like faith—it can increase and become stronger over time. Yet rather than accepting the pace of such never-fast-enough growth, many of us lose heart, decide we can't wait any longer, and take situations into our own hands. When we do so, we lose out on the joy to be found in the close fellowship and the greater dependence on God that come as we wait.

A brief postscript: when God does answer a prayer, His answer may not always be what we expected or even prayed for. Oftentimes it's far better than we could have imagined! Know and believe as you wait for Him to answer your prayers that your heavenly Father will bless you in His perfect ways and perfect time. He *is* faithful!

> *Father, I'm still waiting to hear from You about*
> *_____. Have I missed Your answer?*
> *Align my desires with Yours. After all, You know my*
> *greatest needs better than I do, and I want Your best*
> *for me. . . . Enable me to hear You when You speak. . . .*
> *As I wait, may Your Spirit enable me to be patient.*

NETTING

"I will prevent pests from devouring your crops, and the vines in your
fields will not drop their fruit before it is ripe," says the LORD Almighty.

MALACHI 3:11

Many gardeners are overjoyed when, after they have tended to the vines for a few seasons, berries begin to peek out from their flower caps for the very first time. But if those gardeners aren't careful, the birds will enjoy the berries before they do!

Netting can keep the birds from helping themselves, yet the plant can still grow and the gardeners are still able to view and pick berries. A netted fruit tree, shrub, or bed may not make for an ideal presentation, but the chances of reaping the rewards of one's labor are greatly improved.

This concept of netting reminds me of a verse from Malachi, a book about restoring the relationship between God and His people. During Malachi's time, the hearts and minds of the Israelites were somewhere between complacent and completely turned away from God. The people—including the priests—neglected to tithe (Malachi 3:8). But instead of punishing them, God remained patient; He even offered to protect their crops if they would turn back to Him and offer the full tithe.

Why did the Almighty God insist on the tithe? Of course He doesn't need anything from us—not our money, our time, not even our love—to accomplish His purposes. So in the Israelites' case, He was clearly extending His grace while He patiently allowed them to exercise their free will. But instead of accepting God's offer of protection, the people of Israel arrogantly questioned Him—much as we do today. Like new berries unprotected by netting, the

Israelites turned from God and, without realizing the serious consequences, exposed themselves to unavoidable pestilence and destruction.

Like the Israelites, we also choose to live out from under God's protective umbrella, and as He did in the time of the Israelites, God waits patiently for us to return to Him. When you exercise your free will—a gift from God Himself—freely choose Him. He loves you and wants to bless your life more than you can imagine.

Gracious Father, protect me from those who want to cut off my hope, who want me to turn from You. Thank You for being patient with me despite the ways I reject Your guidance, Your protection, and even Your grace. Thank You for Your steadfast love. I know I don't deserve it.

THE MUSTARD SEED

*"The kingdom of heaven is like a mustard seed that a man planted
in his field. That seed is the smallest of all seeds, but when it grows,
it is one of the largest garden plants. It becomes big enough for
the wild birds to come and build nests in its branches."*

JESUS IN MATTHEW 13:31–32 NCV

S o just how small is the "smallest of all seeds"? About the size of the period
at the end of this sentence. And how big a plant does that tiny mustard
seed become? On average, it grows to nearly eighteen inches tall, a large presence
compared to its tiny beginnings. A mature and firmly-rooted mustard plant is
sturdy enough for birds to build a nest in and flexible enough to sway in the
breeze. Clearly, the growth of the mustard seed was surprisingly disproportion-
ate to its tiny beginnings.

And that's the point Jesus wanted His listeners to understand. Rather than
offering a botany lesson, Jesus wanted the crowd to think about how unexpectedly large the mustard plant is in light of the size of its seed. And that is
how, Jesus wanted them to realize, the kingdom of God would grow. Carpenter-
by-trade and itinerant teacher Jesus of Nazareth first taught twelve unlikely
candidates for preacher/healer/evangelist/church planter. Several were unedu-
cated fishermen; one was a hated tax collector. Yet eleven of the twelve played a
key role in sharing the truth of who Jesus is, and that message has spread around
the world and throughout history for twenty-one centuries. Small seed; unexpectedly huge growth.

That fact is key to another time Jesus referred to a mustard seed: "If you
have faith as small as a mustard seed, you can say to this mountain, 'Move from

here to there,' and it will move. Nothing will be impossible for you" (Matthew 17:20). Here, a small seed resulted in an unexpectedly huge action.

For what seemingly impossible situation do you need a little bit of faith? Think for a moment about the many ways God has been faithful to you. And take some time to count the blessings of the last twenty-four hours. In that context, can you generate a mustard-seed-sized bit of faith? By God's grace, absolutely!

Almighty God, little becomes big in Your hands. What a wonderful truth! I see evidence of this in the growth of Your church and even in my own faith journey. Thank You for growing my faith by being faithful in far greater ways than I would ask or imagine!

MYSTERY PLANT

"The Son of Man came to seek and to save the lost."

LUKE 19:10

Ah, behold the mystery plant! It's that intriguing bulb sitting by itself on a shelf or the plant that is so odd-looking we *have* to purchase it. When it grows, we are always surprised by the results. What we thought was a pepper might be a pumpkin; what we thought was a calla lily turns out to be an iris. Similarly, Jesus saw people we would deem mysterious as the Christ-followers they could become. Zacchaeus is an example.

If you'd asked him that morning, Zacchaeus probably couldn't have explained why he wanted to see Jesus that day. He probably didn't get up that morning and think, *Today I'm going to commit my life to Jesus.* This less-than-honest tax collector—this traitor, this cheat, this bully—knew only that he wanted to see the Rabbi.

So there he was, perched on the branch of a tree, hoping to catch a glimpse of Jesus. Zacchaeus was completely unaware that on this very day Jesus would call him. And that call puzzled Jesus' followers, any one of whom would have gladly hosted Him. But He was going to Zacchaeus's house? Did He know who—and what—Zacchaeus was?

Of course Jesus did—and He chose Zacchaeus anyway. Jesus called this sinner into His kingdom just as He has called you and me. Jesus called Zacchaeus to carry the banner of His holiness, and maybe you were as unsavory a character or at least as unlikely a follower as Zacchaeus was.

And may we learn from the mystery of Zacchaeus's salvation and maybe from the mystery of our own. May these examples prompt us to reach out to the unsavories and the unlikelies, not to be influenced, but to influence. May we befriend them as Jesus did; may we befriend them as someone once befriended you and pointed you to Jesus.

Who needs you to love them in a Christlike way? Take that mystery plant into your heart, let God use you in the growth process, and be blessed by what may be surprising results.

Thank You, Jesus, for the gift of my eternal salvation. Lead me to the Zacchaeuses in my world so that I may show them Your love in gratitude for the grace You have shown me.

NO FORMULA FOR FLOURISHING

The LORD will open up his heavenly storehouse so that the skies send rain on your land at the right time, and he will bless everything you do. You will lend to other nations, but you will not need to borrow from them.

DEUTERONOMY 28:12 NCV

Do you know the kind of gardener who can basically grow a fruit tree from a rock? Gardeners like these don't seem terribly worried about their plants. They might linger on one to check its progress or on another to offer an extra bit of acidifier—and we're puzzled that their garden flourishes. What is their secret? When we ask them, they shrug. Even if they could reduce their gardening to a formula, we would not be guaranteed their level of success. There really are no promises in gardening!

The Lord Jehovah, however, made His people a promise. He didn't offer a magic trick or some trade secret. Instead God spelled out in Deuteronomy 28 the blessings His people would surely receive if they obeyed Him. He called them to work—and to work within His commands—and He promised to bless them when they did.

Yet obedience doesn't come easily, does it? Sin entered the world because we want to live according to our desires, not God's rules. When we recognize the futility of disobedience, we can choose to turn back to Him, confess our sin, receive His forgiveness, acknowledge His sovereignty, and rest in the promise that He will bless our obedience. When Jesus died on the cross, He opened the way for us to commune with our Creator on a deeply personal level, to drink deeply of divine wisdom, and to know peace in the Lord's presence and direction. Intimacy like this cannot be explained, but it can be noticed by people around us.

And when they notice—just as we notice another's amazing garden—we can't offer secrets of success or a magic trick, but we can point them to Jesus. We might also mention that God's blessings on them might look different than the ways He blesses us. And we do well to remind them that God blesses not as a result of a formula or a recipe, but because we are in a relationship with the all-powerful, all-loving God who loves to bless His children.

Lord, thank You for the amazing privilege of being in relationship with You. When people notice the joy and blessings You give me, use me to encourage them to enter into a relationship with You that changes not only each day but eternity as well.

BLOOMS BUT NO FRUIT

[Sinners who have infiltrated your fellowship] are like dirty spots in your special Christian meals you share. They eat with you and have no fear, caring only for themselves. They are clouds without rain, which the wind blows around. They are autumn trees without fruit that are pulled out of the ground. So they are twice dead.

JUDE V. 12 NCV

Few things are more disheartening for vegetable gardeners than seeing their blooming plants produce . . . nothing. In most cases the problem is a lack of pollination, particularly for plants like asparagus or spinach where there may be an imbalance between male or female. But in spiritual matters, the lack of fruit in a believer's life may be due to acceptance of a false gospel, absorption into the ungodly culture, or simply lazy thinking.

Jude described such unproductive believers as "clouds without rain" and "trees without fruit." If we want to produce fruit, we need to filter every new idea through the Lord's truth—we need to be authentic students of the Bible. Too many today are establishing careers rather than pursuing their calling from God, and too many Christians are content to let others tell them what to think rather than be students of the Word themselves. If God's church is to be strong, if God's people are to bear life-giving fruit in this dark and dying world, every one of us needs to know both the Scriptures and the Lord—and no one can do that for us.

Is your church entertaining a new trend, leader, or philosophy that makes you uncomfortable? Ask the Lord to search your heart and reveal if it's because you are resistant to change, or if there is truly something amiss. Check and double-check the matter against God's Word to seek what's true. Be a cloud with rain; be a tree that's deeply rooted and bears much fruit.

Heavenly Father, I'm so thankful for Your Word and the light it shines on any form of darkness. May I be diligent in spending time with You and seeking Your truth for my life. Protect me from influences that aren't of You— from those who aren't sincere in their faith. Lead me in Your righteousness and make my way straight.

MONKEY GRASS

People are tempted when their own evil desire leads them away and
traps them. This desire leads to sin, and then the sin grows and brings
death. My dear brothers and sisters, do not be fooled about this.

JAMES 1:14–16 NCV

Monkey grass is often used to line sidewalks and borders. It's attractive, hardy, and easy to grow. Perhaps a bit too easy. At first, its lush green blades bring immediate gratification; but eventually, the plants thicken and spread and, if not maintained, get out of control. Even when we thin it out and trim it back, monkey grass returns with a vengeance.

The only way to truly be rid of monkey grass is to dig it all up—yank it out, roots and all—and discard it, not leaving a trace where it once flourished. This radical approach is also the only way we can truly rid ourselves of personal sin.

Everyone struggles with personal sin, but what one person finds tempting and troublesome may not be an issue for another. Because it's tailored just for us, our personal sin can be extremely difficult to get rid of. We may start by trying to cut back or limit ourselves, thinking we can control our usual sinful responses. But—as James wrote—let's not be fooled; let's not deceive ourselves. We can't keep ourselves from sinning. Not without God's help. And the longer we go without confessing our sin, the deeper and thicker that deadly plant grows in our heart, becoming harder to overcome.

What personal sin do you need to confess—to dig up, roots and all, and completely get rid of? Ask the Holy Spirit to reveal it. Then confess it and receive God's forgiveness. Trust Him to help you; ask Him to give you His strength to stand against any temptations that would lead to sin.

Holy God, I want to live a life that pleases You. So I ask for Your help. Please reveal to me my unconfessed sin and then show me the steps I need to take to avoid it in my life. On my own I will fail, but with Your help, I know I can stand strong.

STRAW BALE GARDENS

*[Mary] gave birth to her first son. Because there were no rooms left in the inn,
she wrapped the baby with pieces of cloth and laid him in a feeding trough.*

LUKE 2:7 NCV

You may not realize what straw is good for—or even what it's not good for. Essentially, straw is dry, brittle chaff that, unlike hay, has no nutritional value. Straw, however, provides warmth—for animals, sometimes for humans, and even for plants.

From the world's coldest climates to the warmest, straw bale gardens provide a viable alternative for gardeners who want to grow vegetables and herbs but don't have proper soil conditions. In a bale of straw, nutrients and oxygen pass easily to a plant's root system, and water drains properly. Straw bales also provide a warm, insulated, virtually pest- and disease-free environment, protecting plants yet giving them sufficient room to grow.

While the Bible doesn't specifically state that Jesus was placed in a manger filled with straw, it is unlikely that Mary would have placed her tiny baby in a cold, empty manger. Instead, using what they had, Mary and Joseph first protected their baby's soft skin with cloths and then set Him in a bed of straw for added warmth and insulation. The straw-filled manger provided a safe, secure place for a baby to wiggle and a mother not to worry.

Maybe the scene seems very familiar, but try to picture young Mary placing Baby Jesus securely in a straw-filled manger. Imagine Mary and Joseph watching peacefully, staring lovingly at their new Son as He rested, safe and warm.

Now think about the fact that our heavenly Father desires to create the same kind of loving, safe place for us, His children. He wants us to realize that we are only free when we release our worries and cares to Him, when we recognize how helpless we are, when we see that the current climate is too harsh, and when we realize that we can't grow to be the best we can be on our own. We need a Father, we need a Savior, and we need His Spirit to wrap us, cradle us, and place us in His care, even when our circumstances seem like chaff to us.

Lord, I will trust You with my worries and cares. I may not always be excited about the straw bed You place me in, but I will choose to trust that You are keeping me safe and that where I am is indeed the best place for me to grow.

CONTAINER GARDENING

Does not the potter have the right to make out of the same lump of clay
some pottery for special purposes and some for common use?

Romans 9:21

Wander through an urban neighborhood, visit a farm-to-table restaurant, or drive by a food desert, and you will eventually find a few container gardens. These days tubs, barrels, tires, concrete blocks and bricks, milk jugs, shipping pallets, and even satellite dishes are recycled into garden plots. Seeds can germinate, for instance, in small containers, and fruit trees can be happy in large ones. Even very humble-looking containers can house a plant. The creative possibilities are endless. And the same is true for you, as you'll see.

Have you ever been frustrated with the apparent limitations of your life? Have you ever felt insecure about your abilities? If you answered yes to either question, find hope and comfort in Romans 9:21. First, Paul was not saying that some people have a higher calling or greater purpose in life, and the rest of us should settle for a more common lot. The verse offers comfort and hope when we choose to trust that God knows best what roles He's equipped us to fulfill. The boundaries, instructions, and even limitations He has placed in our lives are there for a reason. Be open to the work He has for you to do.

One more note. A plant cannot be moved from container to container and be expected to survive. The only way a root system can mature is within the container where it is planted. Learn from that gardening fact and take heart. Allow yourself to be both at peace and serve as best you can wherever you are today. Your Master Gardener will determine if and when you're due for a transplant.

Lord, I confess that I have not always been open to Your plan for my life. Instead I've been frustrated, often beginning sentences with "If only I had ..." and "It would be different if ...." Help me say, "Because I have ..." and "Because I am ...," so that— wherever You have me planted now—I may be aware of Your presence with me and able to bring glory to Your name.

THE SPIRITUAL GARDEN

*If you faithfully obey the commands I am giving you today—to love the
LORD your God and to serve him with all your heart and with all your soul—
then I will send rain on your land in its season, both autumn and spring
rains, so that you may gather in your grain, new wine and olive oil.*

DEUTERONOMY 11:13–14

Can you imagine a *guaranteed* return on your own gardening efforts? A
guarantee that everything you planted would produce and that your food
supplies would be steady and sufficient every day of the year, whatever the season? Well, we all know that is not the way a garden works!

Look again at the advice in the verse above, a charge God gave the new
nation of Israel, a charge that still holds true today. In the dry, desert land
of Egypt, soil and climate conditions were poor, and the farmers were forced
to transport water to their crops due to lack of rain. Furthermore, since the
Hebrew farmers were Egypt's slaves, it's unclear how much, if any, yield they
would have kept.

Yet here they were, poised to claim the land God had promised them. And
if they showed their love for Him by obeying Him, this nation of Israel would
reap His many blessings.

As long as we live according to our own way, we will not bear fruit that
honors God; we will work but not for any lasting reward. If, however, we live
according to God's instructions, our life will most certainly bear fruit. When
we live in love and obedience to God, when we serve Him and work wholeheart-
edly according to His call, He provides for us: we will never be without spiritual
food and drink. When we walk as His Spirit leads and serve Him with a willing

heart, God promises not always an easy life, but a life filled with His blessing and care.

Lord God, too often I try to tackle life's challenges all by myself. Too often I find myself wanting to control not only the sowing, but the tilling, the growing, and the harvesting as well, instead of waiting for You to instruct me on what You would have me do. Help me to fully surrender to Your ways and to serve You with my whole heart.

PALLET GARDENING

In a wealthy home some utensils are made of gold and silver, and some
are made of wood and clay. The expensive utensils are used for special
occasions, and the cheap ones are for everyday use. If you keep yourself
pure, you will be a special utensil for honorable use. Your life will be clean,
and you will be ready for the Master to use you for every good work.

2 TIMOTHY 2:20–21 NLT

Pallet gardens are exactly what their name suggests: gardens planted on used shipping pallets. Social media sites have blown up with creative ideas for pallet gardens, in part because such plain, utilitarian objects have been repurposed and reborn as homes to lovely microcosms of vegetation and blooms. Restaurants and apartment dwellers especially like these versatile gardens: using the pallets vertically yields protective fencing and landscaping for a patio or balcony.

But as gardeners know, not all pallets are created equal. If a pallet has been pressure-treated with chemicals, it would not be a safe base for a garden. If a pallet is marked "MB," according to the International Plant Protection Convention, it has been treated with methyl bromide and shouldn't be used. Ideally, a gardener wants pallets that have been heat-treated (HT); produced in the United States (two-letter country code: US); and debarked (DB). A pallet with the three recycling arrows is not intended for gardening. Many other symbols exist, but these basics will help you determine if the pallets are safe to use for gardening. If the pallet isn't labeled at all, it's best not to risk using it.

Just as some pallets can be used for gardening, certain utensils have certain uses—as Paul pointed out in today's verse. When we correctly handle

God's Word—when we speak His truth, avoid godless and baseless chatter, and remain true to the Holy Scriptures in our speech and actions—we are vessels of honor that our holy God can and will use for "every good work." Like the pallets with their seals of approval, we can be used by God in His great salvation plan.

Lord Jesus, may I abide in You and in Your Word so that I may recognize godless chatter and false teachings that only confuse hearers rather than point them to You. I want to be a vessel of honor that You can use for Your glory.

ROCK GARDENING

Neither the one who plants nor the one who waters is
anything, but only God, who makes things grow.

1 CORINTHIANS 3:7

Who is the seemingly impossible person in your life whom you must interact with on a regular basis? There's someone like that in everyone's life. Perhaps we work with them, serve with them, gave birth to them, married them, or go to school with them. These people are often socially challenged or just plain self-centered and stubborn. We make various attempts to develop a harmonious relationship, pleading with God to enable us to love this person with His love. Nothing works. Even if we managed to sow a single seed of love, we sense that a hard heart, disinterest, maybe pain, or even fear will keep that seed from growing or even taking root. But just as plants do grow in a rock garden, we may be surprised by what blossoms in a person's hardened heart.

Rock gardens are a great solution to sloping land or other problem areas in a yard. The design and installation take a lot of work, but once they're established, rock gardens are usually very low maintenance. These gardens can also be a great location for more delicate plants that might be overshadowed in a traditional garden. In a rock garden plants have time to develop a root system and grow to maturity with very little disturbance.

In a rock garden, the gardener may pull an occasional weed or periodically water, but nature does its God-given work, and a formerly awkward spot becomes something truly beautiful, if not breathtaking. Gardeners don't need to overhaul the layout or rearrange the rocks in order to uncover the plants' potential. Instead, their unique characteristics are showcased in the new, color-ful growth emerging in the cracks and crannies.

Back to your impossible person. What might happen if you thought of yourself as a seed sower in that impossible person's life? Think too about what may be taking root in his or her heart. Remember that you are in each other's lives for a reason and that God can make things grow in the most unlikely places. If He can create beauty among the rocks, how much more beauty will He bring forth in someone's life?

Lord, You know how difficult it is for me to be around_____—and You know why. Search my heart and help me be a source of encouragement and an example of Your grace when we are together. And when You enable that to happen, to You be all the glory.

THE FORGOTTEN CROP

He causes the grass to grow for the cattle,
And vegetation for the service of man,
That he may bring forth food from the earth . . .
O LORD, how manifold are Your works!
In wisdom You have made them all.
The earth is full of Your possessions.

PSALM 104:14, 24 NKJV

Have you ever unknowingly dropped a watermelon seed on the ground and then, a few months later, discovered a plant growing where you hadn't sown one? You had done nothing to contribute to the vine's growth. In fact, you hadn't even been aware a seed had fallen. Dropped, cast aside, ignored, still this seed somehow managed to thrive. While your intent was never to plant and tend the seed, God had great plans for it.

And the psalmist praised this power of our God. The almighty Creator made all that exists, and it all belongs to Him. We are called to manage and care for His creation—and we pridefully think we do a fine job. But when we discover fruit growing from a stray seed that was thrown out and forgotten, we are reminded that ultimately God is in charge, that the created world is His.

This should give us hope when we are in a season of loneliness or despair, when we truly have no one to turn to. Maybe we're at a new job or just moved to a new city. Maybe we're struggling with an addiction and had to cut ties with old friends as part of our recovery. Maybe we lost someone important to us, or a much-needed and much-loved job, and we find ourselves lacking purpose and hope. But remember that watermelon seed!

As believers, we are never, ever alone: the all-loving, all-powerful Lord is always with us. And the hope we can have because of His love and power can change our perspective on the most dismal of circumstances. When we feel rejected and forgotten, we need to remind ourselves that God is with us and that He is able to do some of His greatest work, whatever the situation, when we are emptiest. Just like that watermelon seed and no matter the odds against us, we can grow in the fullness of God's grace and find new meaning and genuine joy in life.

Precious Father, when I feel alone and hope eludes me, help me remember that You can grow a discarded seed into beautiful fruit. Remind me that all of creation belongs to You and that growth can occur at Your command. I believe; help my unbelief.

A TIME TO REST

*What grows of its own accord of your harvest you shall not reap, nor gather
the grapes of your untended vine, for it is a year of rest for the land.*

LEVITICUS 25:5 NKJV

Gardeners are well aware of the rhythm of the seasons—spring, summer,
fall, winter—and therefore the rhythm of their gardening—plant, tend,
harvest, let alone.

In the book of Leviticus—a book of laws—God introduced to His farming
people an overarching seven-year rhythm. He instructed Israel to plant, prune,
tend to, and harvest crops for six years. In the seventh year, though, the people
were to leave the fields alone. The people were to let weeds grow, let plants die,
and let pests have their way. The land was to have a Sabbath.

In the book of Genesis, God first established this six-one pattern: He
finished His work of creation in six days, and He rested on the seventh day
(Genesis 2:2–3). Then, in the book of Exodus, He instructed His people to follow His example. The third of His Ten Commandments was this: "Remember
the Sabbath day by keeping it holy. Six days you shall labor and do all your
work, but the seventh day is a sabbath to the LORD your God. On it you shall
not do any work" (Exodus 20:8–10).

Taking time for rest and reflection has become a luxury that most of us
think we can no longer afford. Instead, we "tend to one little corner" . . .
and then another . . . and maybe one more . . . until the entire day is filled
with our tending and we miss His blessing and provision. But God set aside
a Sabbath day for our rest and renewal. God Almighty Himself observed the
Sabbath. Then God instructed that His people not only observe a Sabbath for

themselves, but also give their land a Sabbath, a year of rest after six years of producing.

Know that the Sabbath is God's gift to you. Are you receiving His gift of rest for your life?

Holy God, I need to rest in Your warm presence as much as the seeds I plant in my garden need to rest in Your soil and sunshine. I want to learn to honor You by trusting You enough to receive Your gift of the Sabbath, and to truly believe that You will provide for me even as I see You provide for the plants in my garden.

BUTTERFLY GARDENS

The LORD will guide you continually,
giving you water when you are dry
and restoring your strength.
You will be like a well-watered garden,
like an ever-flowing spring.

ISAIAH 58:11 NLT

Who doesn't like a butterfly? These delicate and nimble creatures are both fascinating to watch and interesting to learn about. For starters, butterflies see red, green, and yellow plus a range of ultraviolet colors that are invisible to us. Butterflies use their antennae to sense the air for wind and scents. Many butterflies taste with their feet to determine which leaf is a good place to lay eggs. That choice is important since the caterpillar's diet consists almost exclusively of green leaves. The adult butterfly's diet is liquid, most notably nectar and water. And various butterflies, such as the monarch, are migratory and capable of long-distance flights. Amazing creatures, aren't they?

If you enjoy watching an occasional butterfly flutter by, why not create an environment that attracts many of them? Not only will the flowering gardens beautify your surroundings—including populated urban areas—but they'll also help preserve many species of these graceful and colorful insects.

By including in your garden host plants and nectar plants native to your planting zone, you can observe all four of the mysterious stages of meta-morphosis: egg, larva, pupa, and adult. If, for example, you live in zones 3–9 (eastern North America), the milkweed plant is a must-have. Milkweed leaves are a monarch caterpillar's favorite meal, so mature monarchs prefer to lay their eggs on them. Simply do a bit of research on native plants and butterflies to discover which plants work in your area. You'll find that many of the plants are perennials and can be grown in zones that vary in hardiness. Leaves of asters, snapdragons, sunflowers, and violets are usually quite popular among different species of caterpillars. Nectar plants like black-eyed Susans, Joe Pye weed, and purple coneflower are also sturdy enough to withstand extreme temperatures. Select plants of varying heights and colors, and locate your butterfly garden in full sunlight. You'll attract adult butterflies whether they are seeking nectar or laying eggs.

Once you plant your garden, enjoy hosting one of nature's loveliest displays. Also, though, reflect on how your own heart and home could—like a butterfly garden attracting butterflies—more effectively attract seekers of God's truth and feed people who are spiritually hungry. You will find no better purpose for the garden of your life!

Lord Jesus, thank You for the beauty and complexity of Your creation and how every aspect of Your handiwork points to You. Use my life, I pray, to also point people to You—for their good and Your glory!

HERB GARDENS

*Calling his disciples to him, Jesus said, "Truly I tell you, this poor
widow has put more into the treasury than all the others."*

MARK 12:43

My guess is, if you like to cook, you have homegrown fresh herbs on
hand. Many herbs are simple to grow, and they'll grow just about any-
where—in a windowsill, on a back porch, or in an edible garden, to name a few.
And some herbs—like basil, mint, and thyme—can be used in a wide variety of
dishes. But whether you're making a sauce, a dressing, or an iced fruit drink, a
little bit of an herb goes a long way. A sprig here or a few leaves there can take
the flavor of your dish to a completely new level. A little can be huge!

That was true about the gift of the poor widow we meet in the New
Testament (Mark 12:41–44). Despite the devastating loss of her husband and
the poverty she lived in, this precious woman did not waver in her love for God
or her trust in Him. So when she went to the temple and gave all that she had—
two copper coins worth only a few cents—she did so with a heart full of love
and gratitude. When Jesus noticed her offering, He acknowledged it as greater
than all the money collected that day. She gave so little in the world's eyes, yet
so much in the Lord's because she gave all that she had with a generous, trusting heart of love. Through the gospel of Mark, her example continues to impact
followers of Christ today.

We need the widow's story because we can forget the great impact that
small kindnesses and sacrifices can mean, especially when offered with a humble heart of love. Paying for a stranger's cup of coffee, asking a cashier how she's

doing, holding open a door, or sending a card—these little acts aren't always so little for the one on the receiving end.

Whenever we offer what we have, no matter how small, we are giving far more than that concrete thing. We are giving a taste of God's love, a gift far more valuable than gold.

Lord, when my offering seems small, help me remember
it's not the size of the gift that matters as much as the
sacrifice I'm making and the sincerity in which I'm giving.
May I always be mindful of sharing with others the riches
of Your love, so powerfully illustrated on the cross.

RAIN GARDENS

I have made you pure, but not by fire, as silver is made pure.
I have purified you by giving you troubles.

Isaiah 48:10 NCV

Have you ever seen a shallow depression in someone's yard that's filled with beautiful plants and flowers? Chances are it's a rain garden. The most successful rain gardens are stocked with deep-rooted, native plants that can withstand intermittent watering. The idea is that storm water from roofs, driveways, and other hard surfaces will flow into the rain garden. There, pollutants are both filtered out and broken down by the soil and plants—and kept out of our freshwater supply. Rain gardens reduce the need for irrigation, help purify groundwater, and attract beneficial insects while repelling harmful ones.

Isn't a rain garden a beautiful illustration of the purification process God uses for you and me? As clean, fresh rainwater falls from the clouds, it picks up salt, chemicals, oil, gasoline, and other pollutants. Similarly, you and I pick up sinful ways and worldly habits as we travel through this life. But whenever we turn to Jesus and accept the salvation He offers, we flow into His care. His blood filters out our impurities, and His grace covers our sin. We are cleansed, reminded of our calling to live pure and holy lives, and empowered by the Holy Spirit within us to resist what is harmful and to choose what is beneficial. We are fresh and new once more, like the fresh rainwater in the clouds.

Take a walk through your neighborhood, a local park, or perhaps a business complex that might have a rain garden. Observe the beauty that has emerged in spite of the filth that entered into it. Consider its purpose. Think about what has been salvaged and what is now growing because of this renewal process. Then thank God that He is willing and able to do the same with your heart.

Lord Jesus, thank You for making me clean and pure—for filtering out my sin and impurities and replacing them with Your grace and love. As a result may the beautiful fruit of Your Spirit bloom in my life, attracting others to wonder how this fruit came to be and who my Gardener is!

SOWING TO THE SPIRIT

Whoever sows to please their flesh, from the flesh will reap destruction;
whoever sows to please the Spirit, from the Spirit will reap eternal life.

GALATIANS 6:8

How would you feel if you thought you had planted sunflower seeds but the seeds produced yellow squash instead? There's nothing wrong with yellow squash, but the result would be disappointing. Maybe you had planned to harvest the sunflower seeds, or maybe those sunflowers were an integral part of your companion-planting design. At the least, you had chosen to grow one plant, but a different plant sprouted.

Just like gardeners who have choices about seeds, we have the God-given freedom to make choices about life. Many of these choices may be reduced to two options: we sow either to please ourselves or to please God's Spirit. Just like the supposed sunflower seed that produces a squash, our choice may not be obvious until the fruit appears.

When we want to sow to please the Spirit, we make God essential to our decision making. We seek daily communion with Him by reading Scripture and praying. When we sow to please the Spirit, we also choose a healthy lifestyle—healthy spiritually as well as physically and emotionally. We seek edifying relationships, and we invest our time and energy in edifying activities.

But instructions for our sowing to please God will not always be clearly defined for us. Some decisions will obviously please God, but others take a bit more discernment and prayer. For example, there is nothing wrong with living in a nice home, driving a nice car, taking a vacation, or buying a gift for someone—but what is prompting those uses of our God-given finances? Are we trying to draw attention to ourselves or glorify the Lord? What impact will these purchases have on family time, downtime, our financial support of God's work, and the family's budget? In what way, if any, will these items glorify God?

Other decisions involve not so much the issue itself but whether we handle a given situation in a godly manner. And at still other times, we aren't deciding between right and wrong; our choice is whether to settle for what's good or wait for God's best.

So squash may be delicious, but the gardener intended to harvest sunflowers. Similarly, a life on this planet may be good, but God intends for us to sow "to please the Spirit." How is your crop doing?

Holy God, forgive me for those times I produce
squash when You intend me to sow to the Spirit-
pleasing holiness You designed me to know.

LADYBUGS

Wise people have great power,
and those with knowledge have great strength.

PROVERBS 24:5 NCV

Ladybirds, ladybeetles, ladybugs—they go by a few different names, these bright, beautiful, quiet little bugs that are among some of your garden's greatest defenders and protectors. In fact, it is estimated that one ladybug will consume approximately five thousand aphids in its lifetime—yet these voracious predators gently tickle your finger when, light as a feather, they visit and take a little walk.

Think about some of the ladybugs you may know. Maybe you work with them, maybe you attend church with them, or maybe you're related to them. They are women who quietly protect and provide for their families, friends, church, and community. They may not be loud or very vocal, but they busily act in the best interest of the people they care about. These good-hearted, industrious ladybugs do not wait for someone to tell them what to do or what to think. They consult God and act in accordance with the Holy Spirit's leading. With very little fanfare and never drawing attention to themselves, they accomplish much in God's garden.

Now because these ladybugs quietly go about their tasks, some of us may overlook these women. Or maybe we notice them—they dress too fashionably or not fashionably enough—and dismiss them. If their bright color and industriousness catch our attention, we may think they lack the brainpower needed to discuss serious issues, or they are too serious to be any fun. But when we dismiss the ladybugs in our life, we miss out on some beautiful friendships.

The next time you see a ladybug walking along, place your hand so it will crawl into it. Notice how it doesn't slow its pace or change direction; it is intentional about going where it wants to go, and you can't get it off course. Now think about a lovely ladybug in your life who seems to persevere in the work she is committed to doing. We need these busy ladybugs protecting us and providing for us. We need to learn from and follow their example for the good of our family, friends, church, and community.

Lord, thank You for the ladybugs in my life, for those quietly
industrious women committed to serving You and others.
Help me remember to take notice and give thanks for their
impact in my life and the lives of those around me.

THE RICHES OF REMNANTS

O my people Judah, those of you who have escaped the ravages
of the siege shall become a great nation again; you shall be
rooted deeply in the soil and bear fruit for God.

2 Kings 19:30 TLB

Hold on! Don't throw out that onion stump or potato eye! That's not garbage! That's a new garden waiting to happen!

Many white-root vegetables—fennel, onions, scallions, leeks, lettuces, and
cabbages—often find new life when parts of the plant are placed in shallow
water on a sunny windowsill. Potatoes, ginger, and, in certain zones, even
avocados may be also be renewed. These garden miracles illustrate how God
can renew us.

Many of us can feel like old, discarded scraps for a day or maybe for a
season or, sadly, even for a lifetime if we have experienced trauma or abuse. We
may feel spent, used, too old to make a difference, useless, or trapped. And, in
a sense, we are trapped: our minds and spirits are captives of the enemy, who
has convinced us we are no longer of value. And we would understand if God
disposed of us as easily as we would dispose of a potato eye.

But even when life seems pointless, even when God seems silent, hang on.
Hang on. God intervenes for His children. He steps into our broken lives, He
comforts aching hearts, and He richly applies His healing grace.

When we've been abandoned, hurt, or mistreated—even if the circumstances
are the result of our own wrongdoing—God will keep His promises to us. And
He promised that as long as a remnant of faith remains, He will give root to it
and we will bear His fruit. God is faithful when we are faithless; He is strong

when we are weak; He sees value where the world sees garbage. And He loves us even when we've been deemed—or we have deemed ourselves—unlovable.

What a blessing that God has not given up on us and discarded us!

Father God, thank You for not disposing of me when I am so broken. Thank You for Your faithful love. And thank You for redeeming this pain, for I know that when I am empty, You do some of Your best work in me. Take the pieces of my heart and the pieces of my life, Father, and make me whole and useful once more. Give me roots in Your love that I may bear Your fruit.

STUMPERS

*Paul and those with him went through the areas of Phrygia and
Galatia since the Holy Spirit did not let them preach the Good News
in Asia. When they came near the country of Mysia, they tried to
go into Bithynia, but the Spirit of Jesus did not let them.*

ACTS 16:6–7 NCV

Every gardener has at least one plant that they just can't figure out. It seems to grow—and grow normally and even easily—for everyone else, but not for you. Of course you've followed all the basic gardening rules. You've even consulted experts (in real life and on the Internet). But you're stumped. Adding to the frustration is the fact that your stumper is probably a very common plant, like tomatoes or hydrangeas. *Why isn't this plant growing?!?*

Like our gardens, life also gives us plenty of opportunity to ask "Why?" and plenty of whys that we can't figure out. And these stumpers—a job loss, the sudden death of a loved one, unwarranted criticism, no second date, being left off an invitation list—can be painful or disappointing as well as puzzling.

The apostle Paul experienced such moments. On his first two missionary journeys, Paul planned to enter Asia with the gospel message, but the Holy Spirit did not let him. We don't know how the Holy Spirit halted him, and we really don't know why. But we know that, as he obeyed, Paul had a vision that led him to Macedonia. That redirection, however, doesn't explain why his attempts to enter Asia were thwarted. Eventually, Paul was allowed to enter Asia Minor, and Paul didn't question the messenger or offer us any explanation. He simply accepted the instruction, moved forward in obedience, and actually remained there for some time. And again, we are given no explanation.

Do you handle life's stumpers the way Paul did? Do you accept the change of course and continue to seek God's face? Or do you feel confused or even angry? God always, *always* has our best interest at heart. And He doesn't owe us an explanation for His "nos" and "not nows." In fact, we will never know how many stumpers actually kept us from harm or rerouted us to a place far better than where we were headed. Will you trust God enough to accept life's stumpers with grace?

Gracious God, forgive me for the times I've demanded explanations instead of trusting You, obeying You, and moving forward. I want a faith that isn't rocked by changes but faith that is steadfast and full of hope both in You and in the truth that Your plans for me are good.

BRINGING THE FIRSTFRUITS

We also will bring the firstfruits from our crops and the firstfruits of every tree
to the Temple each year. . . . We will not ignore the Temple of our God.

NEHEMIAH 10:35, 39 NCV

When gardeners collect that first harvest, it is a true victory. They have triumphed over pests, weeds, weather, soil conditions, and vermin; this victory means they will have food. Perhaps others will too. Whoever will benefit, that first harvest is cause for celebration and gratitude.

In Old Testament times, God's people gave the first of their harvests to the people who worked in His temple. This practice not only reminded worshippers to give their best to God and make Him top priority, but it also ensured that those who served in His temple were cared for and fed.

Christians today often honor God with similar gifts of their treasure, talents, and time. Today the financial gifts of God's people support the local church (the staff payroll, the child care workers, the upkeep of buildings, etc.) as well as His mission worldwide (providing the poor with food, clothing, medicine, clean water, homes, and especially hope in Christ). Yet in any given season, we may find it quite challenging to offer any one of these gifts. That's when we do well to consider that our sacrifice involved in giving those gifts pales next to Jesus' ultimate sacrifice of His very life.

Jesus paid the price for your sin and mine, giving us access to heaven for eternity. So, truly, we owe God everything—yet He only asks for a portion. In light of this truth, ask the Lord to guide your gifts of treasure, talent, and time—and then offer those gifts to Him as an act of adoration and appreciation.

Father, I find it difficult to give the church my money when I am financially struggling. . . . I don't even know what talents I have that the church might find useful. And I struggle to commit my time to much of anything these days. Change my heart, I pray, that I may give with gratitude a portion of the treasure, talents, and time You've blessed me with to Your purposes both on this earth and for eternity.

GIFTS FROM THE GARDEN
AND THE HEART

When Ruth rose and went back to work, Boaz commanded his workers,
"Let her gather even around the piles of cut grain. Don't tell her to go
away. In fact, drop some full heads of grain for her from what you have
in your hands, and let her gather them. Don't tell her to stop."

RUTH 2:15–16 NCV

Fresh vegetables from someone's garden or homemade baked goods from a friend's kitchen are always welcome treats. Their thoughtful generosity makes us feel special. The givers didn't need to share, but instead they sought out a person who would enjoy or perhaps truly benefit from their efforts. Consider the ways both Ruth and Boaz selflessly and sacrificially gave what they had to bless others.

Ruth, for instance, gave her loyalty and devotion to her mother-in-law even after she was widowed: Ruth would not let Naomi set out for Judah by herself. And as bitter as Naomi had become after losing her husband and her two sons, she may not have been a very pleasant traveling companion. Boaz too gave beyond what he was required to give. He obeyed God's command to allow the poor to glean from his fields, but when he heard about what Ruth had done for Naomi, his relative by marriage, he wanted to do more for the two women than God required.

Both Ruth and Boaz went beyond God's minimum requirement as they cared for another: their choices model for us selfless and Christlike love. And through Boaz God blessed Ruth and Naomi with more than enough to eat.

Then God blessed the generous Boaz and the loyal Ruth by giving them each other as husband and wife, an outcome neither could have predicted.

Whether we're sharing from God's bountiful blessings or giving to another sacrificially, are we able to act without any concern for personal benefit? Hundreds of years after Ruth and Boaz lived, Jesus made the ultimate sacrifice for you, for me, for all of humankind. And when we care for others out of gratitude for His sacrifice, God will bless that kindness in ways we cannot anticipate nor even imagine. So may we love with Christlike love, not concerned about the cost to us, but trusting God to meet our needs and be glorified in our lives.

Lord Jesus, thank You for paying the debt for my sinfulness. Out of gratitude for that incomparable act of grace, may I live selflessly, act kindly, give joyfully, sacrifice freely, and serve graciously.

YEAR-ROUND HARVEST

There is a time for everything,
and everything on earth has its special season.

ECCLESIASTES 3:1 NCV

Spring and summer are typically thought of as growing seasons, but with more and more people interested in growing their own food, the concept of year-round gardening is catching on.

Yes, with thought, planning, and the right tools, gardening can be done all four seasons of the year. Gardeners, for instance, may rotate in-season plants or use hoop houses or greenhouses. Depending on the garden's location—the Midwest or New England, Texas or the Northwest—some crops may not be as colorful, but they will still feed the gardener. Leafy greens, potatoes, carrots, and peas prefer cooler temperatures, and the add-in color of cool-weather flowers like pansies, crocuses, and primroses keep landscapes vibrant, albeit different from their spring or summer look.

Oh, if only we could tend to our spirits the same way as year-round gardeners. Too often, as a summery spiritual season starts to wane, we slide into complacency, lethargy, and even discouragement. But we have a choice: we don't have to succumb to such end-of-the-season emotions. Instead we can attempt a year-round harvest in our souls. How? Perhaps by asking God to do some crop rotation and greenhousing in our hearts and lives. Maybe, for instance, we find a new way to serve, or we step down from a role in order to get rejuvenated and refreshed. Or perhaps we need to seek forgiveness or extend forgiveness before the spiritual dry spell strangles our zeal. Maybe we need to search out wise counsel for an ongoing problem, or maybe it's time to develop new friendships and interests that draw us into deeper fellowship with Jesus.

Bottom line, we need the Lord. Every morning of our life—no matter the season—we are wise to commit the day to Him. When this becomes a life-giving habit, we may find ourselves better weathering the winter storms and summer-time droughts. We may also find it easier to believe that although our cooler, dormant seasons may not look as vibrant as our springs and summers, the spiritual harvest will still come.

Holy Spirit, prepare me for the cooler spiritual seasons of my life. Provide me with the proper seeds, shelter, and tools so my spirit does not become dormant—and help me release to You any worries about what that season of my life will look like to others. I know that You're in this with me and that You're growing me to be more the person You want me to be.

PLANTING, WATERING, GROWING

*When one says, "I am of Paul," and another, "I am of Apollos," are you
not carnal? Who then is Paul, and who is Apollos, but ministers through
whom you believed, as the Lord gave to each one? I planted, Apollos
watered, but God gave the increase. So then neither he who plants is
anything, nor he who waters, but God who gives the increase.*

4 CORINTHIANS 3:4–7 NKJV

From seed . . . to sprout . . . to seedling . . . from growing plant . . . to blossoming plant . . . to fruit-bearing plant. Gardeners have the tremendous satisfaction of watching this process from start to finish.

Both our perennials and annuals start with a seed that we placed in the soil. Hidden in the protective, nourishing earth, the seed's spark of life awoke at some point and began to grow, roots going down deep and shoot pushing its way through the earth to where sunlight awaited. Once it broke through the surface, we could watch its growth and celebrate even as we did what we could—water and weed, protect from pests and weather—to make that growth happen. Maybe we had a little help in the garden from time to time, but we rightfully felt ownership of our little—or large—plot of land.

Perhaps more like a commercial farm than a homeowner's garden, our spiritual growth is the result of teamwork. Think about the person who first talked to you about Jesus or taught you to sing "Jesus Loves Me." Or maybe you first heard about Jesus when you were older: Who helped you recognize your need for a Savior?

After the seed sowers came some people who, by their prayers and by their teaching, awoke that spark of spiritual life. You may not have been totally aware of the roots you were sending down into God's truth or the growth toward living in His light that you were experiencing. Once you named Jesus your Savior and Lord—once you stepped into life as a Christ-follower—others could not only watch your growth and celebrate, but they could also come alongside you to water and weed and protect, to do what they could to make your relationship with Jesus grow stronger.

Your spiritual growth resulted from teamwork, but none of that teamwork would have been effective if not for God's Holy Spirit. As Paul wrote to the Corinthians, "It is God who gives the increase"! Thanks be to God!

Thank You, Sovereign God, for growing in me a desire to know and love and serve You. Thank You for the many people You put—and continue to put—in my life to encourage my spiritual growth. Use me in Your perfect time and way to encourage the spiritual growth of my brothers and sisters in Christ.

THANKS FOR THE HARVEST

Now may He who supplies seed to the sower, and bread for food,
supply and multiply the seed you have sown and increase the fruits
of your righteousness, while you are enriched in everything for all
liberality, which causes thanksgiving through us to God.

2 CORINTHIANS 9:10–11 NKJV

Stop. Just stop. Stop tilling, stop pulling, stop fertilizing, stop planting, stop plucking, stop pruning, stop fussing, stop clipping, stop worrying. Just stop.

Now sit down . . . right in the middle of your garden patch. Whether yours is a container garden, a vertical garden, a muddy row of corn, a manicured theme garden, whatever it is—sit yourself in it or next to it. Look closely at the plants and marvel at God's handiwork. Touch the plants gently, smell their blooms, and taste their fruit without washing it. Breathe in the garden's essence; exhale the worries of your day. Inhale again, this time letting your soul experience the kind of peace and refreshment that your physical senses just did.

Next, consider that God made this plant. He knows every leaf, petal, seed, and fruit that is there and that ever will be there. God also made the overlooked weed that's right next to the plant you've been focusing on, and He knows all about the weed too. Every plant that grows—each one made by God—has purpose and potential. They blossom, bear fruit, dispense seeds . . . just as we could.

God orchestrated this moment of quiet in your life. Enjoy the stillness; meditate on His goodness; let Him feed your soul in the stillness.

Then, when your heart is so full it could burst, your mind is happily resting in His precious Spirit, and your body is relaxed from His touch, only two words are worthy to break the silence: *Thank You.*

Father of all creation—all that breathes, swims, grows, walks, and crawls—thank You for this beautiful, amazing creation, for the privilege of helping plants grow, and for the lessons You teach me and the peace You bless me with as I garden.

OFFERING THE FRUIT
OF OUR LABOR

Then [Eve] bore again, this time [Cain's] brother Abel. Now Abel
was a keeper of sheep, but Cain was a tiller of the ground. And in the
process of time it came to pass that Cain brought an offering of the
fruit of the ground to the LORD. . . . *but He did not respect Cain and*
his offering. And Cain was very angry, and his countenance fell.

So the LORD *said to Cain, "Why are you angry? And why has your countenance*
fallen? If you do well, will you not be accepted? And if you do not do well,
sin lies at the door. And its desire is for you, but you should rule over it."

GENESIS 4:2–3, 5–7 NKJV

Doesn't it seem as though God treated Cain unfairly? Why would the Lord reject the fresh fruit Cain offered, fruit grown in perhaps the richest, cleanest soil that ever existed outside the garden of Eden? Maybe Cain's offering wasn't what God had asked of him. Maybe it was spoiled or left over from whatever he had reserved for his own consumption. Maybe Cain was bitter, feeling that Abel had the easier, less challenging assignment. Or perhaps Cain—who had done all the hard work involved in planting and tending to the fruit—simply didn't want to share. Whatever his reasoning, Cain was angry and inconsolable after God rejected his offering. That's when God warned him that sin lurked nearby, wanting to consume him, and that he needed to "do well" and "rule over" the temptation to sin.

We need that same warning on our "Cain" days, at those times when we do what we want to do instead of what He has asked or commanded us to do—and then become angry and indignant that He is angry about our disobedience. The next time you are experiencing a Cain day and are feeling angry and insecure, check your motives and your attitudes. If anger is still building, ask the Holy Spirit to give you strength to control it. Remember, sin wants to consume us, but when we cooperate with the Holy Spirit, He won't let that happen.

Holy Spirit, am I doing what God has asked of me—and if so, is my heart attitude right? Or am I thinking I have to work much harder than someone else . . . for less reward? Reveal to me any such sin that is lurking. Help me live for Your approval, always putting forth my best efforts as a way to honor You.

REMAIN IN HIM

"I am the vine; you are the branches. If you remain in me and I in you,
you will bear much fruit; apart from me you can do nothing."

JESUS IN JOHN 15:5

Gardening can challenge even the most expert and most experienced gardeners. Granted, sometimes we bring those challenges on ourselves with our own mistakes, but sometimes the challenges are the result of conditions beyond our control. A gardener, for instance, might try a new soil compound, a new fertilizer, or a new weed control agent only to encounter adverse reactions and unhealthy, sickly plants. Other times pests or disease will threaten a plant's life. Drought, unfavorable temperatures, and flooding can wipe out a season's worth of work. And then there are times when everything's been done "right," but the garden fails, and there is no explanation.

The same things can happen in the garden of our lives. We can work very hard at our jobs, raising our families, and staying in shape physically and spiritually. In some seasons we reap a great harvest, but at other times—maybe due to our mistakes or perhaps because of factors beyond our control—we have little to show for our efforts. Even many seasoned Christians attend church, read a Bible verse each morning, serve on committees, teach Sunday school . . . yet don't experience God's comfort and peace.

Perhaps we are too busy doing these various good things to be truly abiding in the Lord's loving, guiding presence. This is not to say we are to do nothing to grow spiritually. Instead we would be wise to acknowledge our heavenly Father in all that we do. Then, fueled by His divine grace, we can handle with a steadfast spirit our soul-gardening chores as well as whatever outcome He allows.

So if you are weary or totally exhausted—spirit, mind, and body—turn to the Lord. Acknowledge that you can do nothing of eternal value without Him. Ask Him to work in your life and guide your steps so that you will bear much fruit.

Lord, figuratively speaking, I get so caught up in my gardening tasks that I lose sight of You. I cannot do life without You—and I want to stop trying. So in these still, quiet moments, as I listen for Your voice, tell me what You would have me do and where You would have me go. I will follow.

THE PLANT THAT STRUGGLED

*"There will be more joy in heaven over one sinner who repents than
over ninety-nine just persons who need no repentance."*

JESUS IN LUKE 15:7 NKJV

I can only imagine being a gardener in Eden, in that place of perfect seeds and soil and weather. What a different experience from, for instance, planting fifty pepper plants and having one begin to yellow and wilt within a couple days. When something like that happens, I check the soil, try to determine if it's overhydrated or dehydrated, add fertilizer, and look for evidence of pests as it continues to wither and turn brown. But then, suddenly, new leaves appear, and I am overjoyed to see tiny green buds protruding slightly from the shoot. For reasons only the Master Gardener knows, the pepper plant begins to thrive.

Why am I so thrilled about that once-sickly plant when I have so many healthy plants? One reason is that I had invested time and energy in that plant. When it came back from the brink of death, I couldn't help but be joyful.

Jesus knows the far greater joy of having the one lost soul in a group of His followers return to Him. It's not that He thinks less—or less often—of those followers who are strongly rooted in the faith; it's that He wants all to be saved and able to spend eternity with Him. Those individuals who have declared their faith in Him are already safe in His care; the sinner whose soul remains lost is the person with the greater need.

As believers, we are to stand beside lost individuals, form a genuine relationship that encourages their growth, and allow them to rely on us for whatever support they need. As the Lord uses us to revive the withering plant—or, to mix metaphors, to search for the missing sheep—may we be mindful that those who are saved will be saved for reasons only the Master Gardener, only our good Shepherd, knows. As He does His job, we will be doing ours by showing them the same love that people showed us when we were withering or lost.

Lord Jesus, I want to love with Your love those souls that are withering or lost. Enable me to remove any prejudices, judgments, and assumptions from my heart so that I may see them as You do: glorious and beloved children of the Father who have the opportunity for eternal life with Him. Remind me that You love them as much as You do me, and that at some point, You used someone to revive me as I withered and to bring me into Your flock when I was lost.

THE SOILS

"When the sun was up [the seeds] were scorched, and because they
had no root they withered away. And some fell among thorns, and the
thorns sprang up and choked them. But others fell on good ground and
yielded a crop: some a hundredfold, some sixty, some thirty."

MATTHEW 13:6–8 NKJV

Clearly, Jesus the Carpenter understood some basics about gardening. Sometimes seeds are dried up before they sprout, take root, and grow. Sometimes young seedlings are choked out by older, already-established plants. And of course seeds do best "on good ground."

Jesus, however, was not merely talking about horticulture. He was teaching about spiritual growth: the seed of the gospel—the all-important truth that Jesus is God's Son, who came to this earth to take our punishment for our sin so that we can know God's forgiveness, adoption into His family, and eternal life with Him—can change a life for eternity if we open our heart, receive that seed, and allow it to take root.

The world can distract us, preventing us from tending to the garden of our soul. If we don't water our newly planted seed of truth, it will not take root. Or if we have watered that seed and seen it sprout, we must be careful not to let it get choked out by life's pressures and responsibilities, pain and disappointments. Then there's the good soil—and, interestingly, nothing improves the quality of soil like manure.

This reality may be counterintuitive, but the hard times of life, the loss that stuns, the pain that sears—these can enrich the soil of our heart and grow our faith. Experiences we would never choose for ourselves and seemingly never-ending seasons of darkness are made sweet when we know God's presence with us in a more real way than ever before.

Whether your seed of the gospel is a seedling, a sprout, or an established plant, continue watering it with God's truth. Protect it and nourish it so that when the hard times come, those times will be fertilizer that enriches a heart committed to God.

Lord God, I look to you with faith and hope that You
can and will use the dark and painful times of my
life to grow a deeper relationship with You.

GROWING AS GOD INTENDED

She inspects a field and buys it.
With money she earned, she plants a vineyard.

PROVERBS 31:16 NCV

In today's verse, taken from the Proverbs 31 description of a wife of noble character, the poet speaks on God's behalf and praises the woman's business savvy and work ethic. She herself has inspected a field and purchased it: she didn't buy it impulsively, nor expect a man to do it for her. She studied the soil conditions and developed a strategy for its best use. She planted the vineyard rather than wait for someone to do it for her. We can only assume the vineyard was successful, because this woman puts much thought and care into her endeavors.

Along the way, though, some people have either dismissed as outdated or conveniently forgotten this woman in Proverbs 31 who admirably uses her brain and gets her hands dirty in order to accomplish her goals. Somewhere along the way, our Christian culture started to regard women who have careers and women don't mind doing yard work, changing a tire, or unclogging a toilet as less feminine or as not fulfilling some biblical definition of womanhood. Proverbs 31:16 should clarify for all of us that women are to use their minds, be free to make sound business decisions, have no fear about rolling up their sleeves, and make no apologies for their accomplishments.

You may be a whiz at retirement investments but a complete disaster in the kitchen. You may be able to install a new electrical outlet, but you too often add bleach instead of fabric softener to your laundry. Despite the burned biscuits and ruined shirts, never let anyone suggest you are less of a woman because you do not fit some misguided stereotype. The Bible praises a woman who is strong and unafraid to use her God-given talents—whatever those may be. So don't hesitate to kill the bug, bring home the check that pays the mortgage, and buy that new ratchet set you've been eyeing.

Father, thank You for wiring me with a unique combination of gifts and attributes. And rather than letting anyone else define womanhood or determine my value, may I rest in the truth that You created me and You love me.

THE SOWER

[Jesus] spoke many things to [the crowd] in parables, saying: "Behold, a sower went out to sow. And as he sowed, some seed fell by the wayside; and the birds came and devoured them. . . . He who has ears to hear, let him hear!"

MATTHEW 13:3–4, 9 NKJV

You have just read the beginning and end of the parable of the sower, sometimes called the parable of the soils. Both titles fit because this story reassures sowers about their efforts and also describes the results of seeds sown in different soils. The seed is the gospel; the soils are the different responses of those who hear that message.

Consider the sower for a moment. First, the context in this sowing is the Great Commission—and the Great Commission is not a suggestion or request. It is a commandment from Christ Himself that each of us is to obey. And each of us has probably, in response, gone out with the gospel message—and then felt like utter failures when the response was not an immediate and fervent conversion evident in the person's on-fire zeal for the Lord.

So Jesus' words in this parable offer relief when we're discouraged by the apparent ineffectiveness of our sowing. We see in this story, however, that we are responsible for carrying the gospel message, but we cannot be responsible for how people respond. If we find ourselves disappointed time and again when we share our faith, maybe our focus has slipped. Maybe we're disappointed that *our* message wasn't well-received and that the response didn't make *us* look good. But in this parable—and elsewhere in scripture—Christ taught that some people simply will not hear, that the messenger is not always welcome, and that the gospel message will not always be well received. In other words, you and I are off the hook when it comes to saving souls; that specific role belongs solely to the Lord.

Then, for those fervent evangelists among us, this parable offers biblical support for not turning a conversation about sin and salvation into a pressure cooker; for those of us who are shy, this parable frees us to share the good news without worry. There are no magic words, surefire formulas, or special pieces of equipment involved. We simply and straightforwardly share Jesus with others—and that's it.

What seeds will you sow today?

Lord Jesus, thank You for reminding me that I sow seeds, but You tend to them. I will not always know or understand the outcome of my sowing—but not knowing is part of Your plan. Strengthen me, I ask, in the role of the sower and keep me ever mindful that You are the Gardener.

THE COMMAND OF THE AGES

The LORD God took the man and put him in the Garden
of Eden to work it and take care of it.

GENESIS 2:15

We all know what happened next. . . . Adam and Eve sinned, they were ultimately banished from God's garden, and gardeners have been fighting pests, droughts, and floods ever since.

No one knows the garden of Eden's exact location, but we do know it was a place of peace, plenty, and purpose. And God handed this portion of the world He created to His prize creation—mankind—to manage. God intended for us to care for His land before sin entered the world, and it was His command after the fall as well. Once sin infected all of creation, however, the task became far more difficult.

Natural resources that used to exist in abundance are now more limited and therefore more expensive. Recycling efforts are hardly universal, and debates continue over its cost-effectiveness. Nourishing the soil organically is costly and time consuming. And too many generations have left much-needed conservation, maintenance, and cleanup to the next generation. With so much waste and filth built up, it's overwhelming to think about saving this polluted planet.

Yet we are to care for God's creation because He commanded us to however difficult the task becomes. When we humbly accept this demanding role as caretakers on behalf of the Creator, we experience a deep satisfaction in knowing we are pleasing Him with our efforts. After all, it's His creation.

Caring for the earth—beginning in our own backyards—can be a worshipful response of both love for God and gratitude for this stunningly beautiful planet on which we live. Regardless of what our personal effort might yield, we can be certain that when we serve as God commanded, the harvest in our hearts will be peace, plenty, and purpose.

Lord, thank You for the opportunity to be a caretaker of Your beautiful creation. Show me how to be a good steward of the natural resources You've provided. And know that I long to grow closer to You even as I help care for Your mighty handiwork.